101 E

FOR SECC

101 ESSENTIAL LISTS SERIES

101 ESSENTIAL LISTS
FOR SECONDARY
TEACHERS

Susan Elkin

continuum
LONDON • NEW YORK

Continuum International Publishing Group
The Tower Building   80 Maiden Lane
11 York Road   Suite 704
London   New York
SE1 7NX   NY 10038

www.continuumbooks.com

British Library Cataloguing-in-Publication Data
A catalogue record for this book is available from the British Library.

ISBN: 0-8264-8870-6 (paperback)

Library of Congress Cataloguing-in-Publication Data
A catalog record for this book is available from the Library of Congress.

Typeset by YHT Ltd
Printed and bound in Great Britain by Ashford Colour Press Ltd,
Gosport, Hampshire

CONTENTS

Personal Matters

LIST 1   Curriculum vitae

- Your curriculum vitae (CV) is your professional shop window. It shows:
  - who you are
  - what you are
  - what you've done.
- Put your CV on a computer. Update it whenever you achieve anything significant or your circumstances change. Then, when you need to show it to anyone, you can simply email it to them or run off a paper copy. Ideally it shouldn't cover more than two sides of A4 paper.
- Include on it all the jobs you've had and the posts you've held, with dates.
- List your qualifications, with dates and awarding bodies. Don't forget those other relevant achievements either. If you happen to be a Grade 8 pianist, a qualified swimming instructor or hold a licence to drive a motor coach, then say so.
- Don't forget your full contact details: home address, phone number (landline and mobile) and email address.
- Put in any other skill-developing activities, such as leading in-service training (INSET), sitting on working parties, organizing events or writing curriculum materials.
- Briefly list your personal out-of-school interests, such as golf, dog-breeding, reading, theatre, motor bikes or whatever. It adds to the picture of you as a whole person.
- Adapt the basic CV for different purposes. If, for instance, you're applying for an advisory teacher's secondment with your LEA, it would make sense to emphasize the professional development work you've led with colleagues. A CV that accompanies an application for a subject-based post should stress subject expertise and experience. The simplest way to manage this is to copy your basic CV onto a new blank document on the computer and then adapt it while keeping the original intact for next time.

L I S T 2 Health

Secondary schools are tough, complex places to work in. You teach a range of classes and some of them can be very challenging. Don't run risks with your health or you might find it all gets too much for you. Besides, you want to feel chirpy enough to enjoy the weekends and holidays. So:

○ Eat breakfast. Fruit, wholemeal toast, sugar-free muesli and plain yoghurt are all simple and quick to prepare at home. Alternatively, eat something healthy in the school dining room if it serves breakfast.

○ Eat lunch and allow yourself time to chew it. A simple sandwich with nutritious ingredients such as salad really doesn't take long to make and pack. You could buy something at school. There is nothing clever or 'macho' about teachers who say, 'Oh I never stop for lunch'. It's bad management, not something to be proud of. Their afternoon classes suffer. Lunch is an essential, not a luxury.

○ Get some exercise each day. A short walk with the dog before or after school works wonders. Consider becoming an early morning swimmer. Most areas have a pool offering pre-work sessions and it can really perk you up for the day.

○ You are a role model for your teenage pupils – don't be tempted to drive between the school's buildings.

○ Watch your posture. Walk tall.

○ Bend from the knees, not the waist, when you drop the electronic board marker pen on the floor. Many teachers take time off every year with (avoidable) back injuries.

○ If stress is a problem, try deep breathing slowly from the diaphragm.

○ Keep to a reasonable bedtime. Sleep is vital to health.

○ If you have difficulty getting to, or staying, asleep try:
  - a hot bath with lavender oil before bedtime
  - a milky drink at bedtime
  - not doing any school work of any kind for at least two hours before bed
  - taking an early evening walk
  - sex
  - consulting a doctor or a sleep expert
  - seeking advice from one of the many available books or websites on insomnia.

L I S T 3   **Pensions**

Keep an eye on what's likely to be in the pot for you when you retire. Don't assume that if you're only 22 it doesn't matter. Trust me – it does.

○ Deductions are made from your salary ('superannuation') towards your pension if you're full-time in a mainstream school, but may not be if you:
  - teach only on supply basis
  - work only on short contracts
  - teach in an independent school.
○ You can top up your future pension by paying additional voluntary contributions (AVCs) on a monthly basis.
○ Check your position with Teachers' Pensions, Mowden Hall, Darlington DL3 9EE. Tel: 0845 6066166; Web: www.teacherspensions.co.uk.
○ Consider taking out a private – probably 'stakeholder' – pension as an additional investment. Your contributions are tax deductible.
○ Consult your professional organization (see List 5 Joining a union). All the teaching unions offer pensions advice for members.
○ Seek advice from an independent financial adviser. Remember that for real independence you will have to pay a fee. If the service is free it's because the adviser is on commission from a finance company and the advice cannot, therefore, be impartial. Find one via the Association of Independent Financial Advisers, Austin Friars House, 2–6 Austin Friars, London EC2N 2HD. Tel: 020 7628 1287; Web: www.aifa.net.

LIST 4 Those long holidays

Let's be honest, although it may not be what we admit to non-teaching friends in the pub, one of the best things about this job is the long holidays. Most secondary schools still have six weeks off in the summer. Some independent schools have more. And even if you're in a school or LEA running a four-, five- or six-term year you will still get at least a month off in the summer. So:

○ make the most of the break
○ do anything you really have to do immediately after you break up.

Then *forget* school! And don't:

○ waste that glorious stretch feeling guilty about school and doing, or pretending to do, schoolwork
○ bore everyone near you with tales of how much work you have to do.

Any of these 'projects' appeal?

○ Camp or caravan with the children in France.
○ Walk a long distance footpath such as the Pennine or North Downs Way.
○ Go to Florence to study Italian at the British Institute (www.britishinstitute.it).
○ Explore the US using the cheap and efficient Greyhound buses (www.greyhound.com).
○ Curl up in the garden or sitting room with all the books that haven't been read since the previous summer.
○ Write a book.
○ Decorate the house throughout.

L I S T
5

Joining a union

We live in a litigious age and secondary pupils are volatile young adults. You need to know that there's a source of impartial help and advice behind you and one which will also get you a lawyer in an emergency. Even if you don't see yourself as a trade union type, think of it as insurance. You can claim the annual membership fee as a deductible expense on your tax return.

○ Association of Teachers and Lecturers (ATL): 7 Northumberland Street, London WC2N 5RD. Tel: 020 7930 6441; Web: www.atl.org.uk; Email: info@atl.org.uk.
○ National Association of Schoolmasters Union of Women Teachers (NASUWT): Hillscourt Education Centre, Rose Hill, Rednal, Birmingham B45 8RS. Tel: 0121 453 6150; Web: www.teachersunion.org.uk; Email: nasuwt@mail.nasuwt.org.uk.
○ National Union of Teachers (NUT): Hamilton House, Mabledon Place, London WC1H 9BD. Tel: 020 7388 6191; Web: www.data.teachers.org.uk.
○ Professional Association of Teachers (PAT): 2 St James' Court, Friar Gate, Derby DE1 1BT. Tel: 01332 372337; Web: www.pat.org.uk; Email: membership@pat.org.uk.

Joining a subject association

Secondary school teachers are subject specialists. Keep up to date with your subject knowledge and teaching by joining a subject association.

- National Association for the Teaching of English: 50 Broadfield Road, Sheffield S8 0XJ. Tel: 0114 255 5419; Web: www.nate.org.uk; Email: info@nate.org.uk.
- Association of Teachers of Mathematics: Unit 7 Prime Industrial Park, Shaftesbury Street, Derby DE23 8YB. Tel: 01332 346599; Web: www.atm.org.uk; Email: admin@atm.org.uk.
- The Association for Science Education: College Lane, Hatfield, Hertfordshire AL10 9AA. Tel: 01707 283000; Web: www.ase.org.uk; Email: info@ase.org.uk.
- The Geographical Association: 160 Solly Street, Sheffield S1 4BF. Tel: 0114 296 0088; Web: www.geography.org.uk; Email: ga@geography.org.uk.
- The Historical Association: 59a Kennington Park Road, London SE11 4JH. Tel: 020 7735 3901; Web: www.history.org.uk; Email: enquiry@history.org.uk.
- National Association of Music Educators: Gordon Lodge, Snitterton Road, Matlock, Derbyshire DE4 3LZ. Tel: 01629 760791; Web: www.name2.org.uk.
- National Society for Education in Art and Design: The Gatehouse, Corsham Court, Corsham, Wiltshire SN13 0BZ. Tel: 01249 714825; Web: www.nsead.org.
- The Professional Council for Religious Education: 1020 Bristol Road, Selly Oak, Birmingham B29 6LB. Tel: 0121 472 4242; Web: www.pcfre.org.uk; Email: retoday@retoday.org.uk.
- The Association for Language Learning: 150 Railway Terrace, Rugby CV21 3HN. Tel: 01788 546443; Web: www.all-languages.org.uk; Email: info@all-languages.org.uk.
- The Physical Education Association of the United Kingdom: Ling House, Building 25, London Road, Reading RG1 5AQ. Tel: 0118 378 6240; Web: www.pea.uk.com; Email: enquiries@pea.uk.com.
- Association for ICT in Education. Tel: 01708 433822; Web: www.acitt.org.uk; Email: membership@acitt.org.uk.
- The Design and Technology Association: 16 Wellesbourne House, Walton Road, Wellesbourne, Warwickshire CV35 9JB. Tel: 01789 470007; Web: http://web.data.org.uk.

- The Association for Citizenship Teaching: 63 Gee Street, London ECIV 3RS. Tel: 020 7566 4133; Web: www.teachingcitizenship.org.uk; Email: info@teachingcitizenship.org.uk
- National Association of Careers and Guidance Teachers: Tel: 01295 720809; Web: www.nacgt.org.uk.

Pursuing your hobbies and calling it work

One of the joys of teaching is that, whatever your personal interests and passions, you can (providing they're legal!) build them into extra-curricular work with pupils irrespective of what your subject is. For the pupils it also helps to break down stereotypical images if, for example, a science teacher plays the cello in the school orchestra or an art specialist coaches football. In other words, there's scope for doing your own thing and pretending it's work. 'Enrichment' activities undertaken by teacher enthusiasts in schools I have visited include:

○ chess club
○ embroidery
○ writing the school pantomime
○ close harmony singing
○ abseiling club
○ cricket coaching
○ cookery club
○ reading club
○ rugby refereeing
○ string quartet
○ quizzes
○ jazz band
○ Latin club
○ directing plays
○ writing musicals
○ Italian club.

LIST 8 — Moonlighting

Many secondary teachers make extra money by diversifying at weekends and during holidays, by exploiting subject specialisms and skills or by cashing in on a hobby. Some find that having a second occupation – doing something they really like – helps with stress and insularity. A modest top-up income helps too. What can *you* do? I have met secondary teachers who moonlight in all these jobs:

○ folk fiddler
○ puppeteer
○ bookmaker
○ tenor soloist for classical concerts
○ after-dinner speaker
○ maker of quiches for local health food shop
○ gardener
○ tourist guide
○ freelance journalist
○ novelist
○ quiz-setter
○ translator
○ creator of celebration cakes
○ wedding-dress designer
○ wood turner
○ proofreader
○ clothes retailer holding 'parties' in customers' homes.

Be Prepared 2

LIST 9   Your essential kit

Never arrive at a lesson without:

- spare pens and pencils for pupils who have forgotten theirs
- a few erasers and pencil sharpeners
- marker pens for the whiteboard (or chalk for the blackboard if the school's still in the dark ages)
- cloth for cleaning the whiteboard (or blackboard rubber)
- spare copies of any books you'll be using – even if the pupils have been issued with take-away copies, some will have forgotten them
- a packet of file paper
- a box of tissues
- a pile of commendation slips, if that's the school's reward system for good work, behaviour, etc.

You may have a designated room where you teach most of the time, in which case you can probably leave some of these things in it. But if colleagues are sometimes timetabled to use 'your' room, such everyday items will grow legs and walk, so have supplies in your bag too. It's even more important if you are timetabled in various rooms during the week.

L I S T 10 Tips for lesson preparation

- Find all the resources you need in advance.
- Have duplicate copies of books, CDs and so on at home so that you can prepare these without having to carry a lot of equipment backwards and forwards.
- Make a note of page numbers in books and exact locations on CD-ROMs, videos, DVDs and websites that you'll want the class to look at.
- Make brief notes to remind yourself what you're going to say at the beginning of the lesson – perhaps the introduction of a topic.
- In theory, every lesson should have a beginning, a middle and a neat end. In practice, many lessons are simply a continuation of 'what we were doing yesterday', so don't spend too much time worrying about this.
- If you've asked the pupils to read something for homework, make sure you have re-read it for the lesson so that you can question them closely on it.
- File your notes and materials carefully. You will probably be able to use the same lesson with the equivalent class(es) next year. You don't want to be re-inventing the wheel every week for the rest of your career.
- Keep one large ringbinder of cumulative lesson notes for each class you teach.
- If you've got an electronic whiteboard in the classroom, consider the use of PowerPoint for some lessons. Then file the material carefully for next time.

Have a short story handy

Almost all young people like, and benefit from, being read to. You can often quell even the most potentially riotous of groups with a well-chosen short story. This is especially useful when:

○ you find yourself 'covering' a class for a subject you know nothing about and for which no work has been left
○ your class has finished its work and you have ten minutes to fill at the end of a lesson
○ it's Friday or the end of term and you and the pupils think you've earned a treat
○ you've left your briefcase containing your carefully prepared lessons on the train.

The following are usually hits across the secondary school age group and one or two of them have been known to reduce hardened, towering, testosterone-filled teenage boys to tears:

○ 'Spit Nolan' and 'Seventeen Oranges', *Goalkeeper's Revenge* by Bill Naughton
○ 'The Elephant's Child', *The Just So Stories* by Rudyard Kipling
○ 'Royal Jelly' by Roald Dahl, first published in *Kiss Kiss* but reproduced in various other sets of Dahl short stories
○ 'The Gift' by Hugh Oliver, *An Oxford Book of Christmas Stories* (ed. Dennis Pepper)
○ 'Indian Camp' by Ernest Hemingway, first published in *The First Forty-Nine Stories* and reproduced in *Modern Short Stories* (ed. Jim Hunter)
○ 'The Daughter' by Jacqueline Wilson, *Centuries of Stories* (ed. Wendy Cooling).

Word wheels at the ready

If you need to occupy a class for a few minutes unexpectedly or you have a few minutes to fill, give them a word wheel to do, linked to the subject of the lesson.

Choose a seven-, eight- or nine-letter word. Draw a wheel with spokes on the board. Put one letter in the centre and each of the others, out of order, in one of the surrounding empty wedges. The task is to make as many words as possible of three letters and more using only the letters on the wheel – and to find the whole word. Every word must include the centre letter. For example:

In English use SEMICOLON (E in centre)

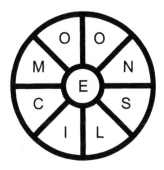

Here are some words to start you off (alert pupils will find more):
cine, cone, come, close, isle, lemon, line, lime, lice, lone, mine, mice, mile, nice, omen, once, slice, clime, since.

- Maths: ESTIMATE (M in centre), CALCULATE (C in centre), TANGENT (N in centre)
- Science: HYDROGEN (E in centre), LEVERAGE (R in centre), PIPETTE (I in centre)
- Geography: GLACIER (C in centre), ARGENTINA (N in centre), DOLOMITES (T in centre)
- History: CONQUEST (S in centre) ELIZABETH (E in centre), EVIDENCE (D in centre)
- Music: CLARINET (R in centre), CONCERT (E in centre), SEMIBREVE (S in centre)

- RE: MORALITY (O in centre), BIBLICAL (I in centre), MEDITATE (T in centre)
- D&T: DESIGNER (G in centre), WORKSHOP (P in centre), MATERIAL (E in centre)
- PE: NETBALL (B in centre), EXERCISE (C in centre), TRAINER (R in centre).

In a French, Spanish or other modern-language lessons do it in the relevant language, e.g. MONSIEUR, CROISSANT, RELACION, ORDENADOR, KARTOFFEL, EINGANG.

An elimination puzzle in your bag

An elimination puzzle is an uneven number of apparently random words which the solver, given clues, crosses off in pairs. Eventually one word will be left over and that's the answer. This needs a bit of preparation. Make up some of these and put them on a computer, then it really is quite simple to run enough off for each member of the class when you need them and you can use them over and over again with different classes. Elimination puzzles can be based on any subject. This example is for a geography lesson. Let them use atlases, etc., to find answers they don't know.

Cross off two of these 21 words for each of the 10 clues below. The answer to the puzzle is the one word left over.

Bed, Contour, Darling, Don, End, Fin, Good, Granite, Hope, Isle, Land, Limestone, Line, New, Red, River, Sea, South, Snow, Tweed, York.

1 Separates Egypt from Arabian Peninsula
2 US city
3 Two rocks
4 English seaside town
5 Two rivers
6 Its capital city is Helsinki
7 Highest peak in Wales
8 Bottom of a water course
9 Cape at southernmost tip of Africa
10 Links places of equal height on a map.

Answers: 1 Red Sea 2 New York 3 Granite and limestone 4 Southend 5 Darling and Tweed 6 Finland 7 Snowdon 8 River bed 9 Good Hope 10 Contour line. Overall answer: Isle.

Have an assembly up your sleeve

One day you will arrive at school and find that a flu epidemic or some other crisis has caused large-scale teacher absence – and there is no one available to take assembly except you. Instant assemblies for emergencies:

○ 'The Good Samaritan' (*The Bible*, St Luke, chapter 10 verses 30–5). Draw moral points about kindness and how important it is to avoid stereotyping.

○ Use an anecdote from your own childhood and draw some moral/learning/useful points from it (e.g. when my friend was badly burned by a firework or when my neighbour got a bravery award).

○ Take a story about courage, etc., from that morning's newspaper. Read it aloud and comment on it.

○ Let us be thankful for . . . Take something which pleases you and spend a few minutes explaining why and commenting on its benefits. For example, you might celebrate:
  - the quirks of English language, such as proverbs, quotations, unusual words or dialects
  - our weather
  - loving pets (tell them about yours – this always goes down well!)
  - books
  - TV
  - football.

I once heard a desperate deputy head do an entire off-the-cuff assembly for the whole school on the joys of horse chestnut trees. Just think laterally!

L I S T 15 Have in your locker...

○ Two or three mugs for tea and coffee.
○ A jar of coffee and/or teabags.
○ Sugar, if you're likely to want it.
○ Aspirin or Paracetamol.
○ Lost-voice remedy, e.g. Vocalzone.
○ Muesli bars for a healthy snack if you have to stay late or you missed breakfast.
○ A spare pair of glasses if you're a spectacles wearer.
○ A spare pair of tights (women).
○ Safety pins.
○ A fleece, jacket or jumper in case you end up on unexpected outdoor supervision.
○ A spare tie in case you spill something down yours (men).
○ Sanitary towels, tampons, etc. (women).
○ A good book in case you ever get stuck at school and actually have time to spare, say between the end of lessons and the start of a parents' evening. It has been known!

LIST 16   **What not to wear**

Dressing for secondary school teaching can be a minefield, especially for women who should be aware that their clothes will be scrutinized minutely by the girls, and certain clothing can give teenage boys the wrong signals. Moreover it's a workplace and you want to give the young adults in your charge the right messages. So:

○ Find out if there's a formal school dress code and follow it.

○ Even if there isn't a formal code there will be an informal one. Look closely at what others are wearing and blend in, but don't model yourself on obvious mavericks such as that tattooed chap in the drama department with stripy hair who always wears patched jeans and a flowing cerise tunic top.

○ If you're male you may be expected to wear a collar, tie, jacket or even a suit.

○ If you're female, 'office dress' may be the norm.

○ If you're in the PE department, or if you teach a 'messy' subject such as art, you will obviously need specific clothing for your subject, but some schools will expect you to dress conventionally for formal occasions such as assemblies and parents' meetings.

○ For good discipline it's sensible to go easy on the jewellery and make-up which the pupils aren't allowed to wear. If the girls are forbidden large dangly earrings or facial studs, you will form a better rapport with them if you keep your earrings small and leave your nose stud at home.

○ If you're female and working with teenage boys avoid: very short skirts, skirts with slit sides, low-cut tops, skimpy dresses, low-cut trousers which expose the waist and very tight trousers or leggings.

Dealing with Emergencies

3

L I S T 17   Fire

○ You *must* know exactly what the school's fire procedure is – even if you're only there for a single day in a supply capacity.

○ You *must* know where the nearest fire exit and muster point is for every room you teach in or public area of the school (e.g. the hall) that you use.

If you're in the middle of a lesson when the fire alarm goes:

○ stop what you're doing immediately

○ always assume maximum seriousness even when you know in advance that it's only a drill (you won't always know)

○ insist on total silence

○ follow the school's policy closely, e.g. close the classroom windows

○ get the class out of the room and to the fire exit and muster point as quickly as you can, but don't allow any running

○ demonstrate by your own behaviour that the fire bell signals something serious and potentially life-threatening

○ exercise common sense

○ be calm (outwardly at least).

I once taught in a London school in which a major fire broke out while the school was in session. It took several fire engines a long time to get it under control and one staircase was unusable. These things really do happen. Fortunately, on that occasion, everyone was evacuated safely.

L I S T 18   Pupil illness

There are young people in every secondary school suffering from serious conditions such as epilepsy, diabetes and asthma. All schools have systems for giving teachers essential and confidential information about these pupils. Make sure you check the list scrupulously so that you know if any pupil in any of your classes has an ongoing condition and you are confident of what you should do in an emergency.

○ If a pupil with a known ongoing condition is taken ill – such as an asthmatic having an attack or an epileptic going into a fit – make sure you:
  - keep calm
  - follow the procedures laid down for that particular child
  - don't allow others to crowd round
  - send another pupil to get help from school first-aider/nurse/ doctor
  - heed the sufferer's own instincts. He or she is used to dealing with this condition, you're not
  - take the sufferer out of the room, if appropriate, or arrange for a colleague to take the rest of the class out. Either way you need help, so send for it immediately.
○ For more minor incidents:
  - if a child says he/she is going to be sick, let them go to the toilets immediately. Send a friend to investigate after a few minutes. (The last thing you want is anyone throwing up on the classroom floor!)
  - be gentle with, and keep an eye on, a pupil who complains of a headache or stomach ache
  - if the problem persists, send the sufferer to the medical room with a friend as escort
  - make sure you know what the school's procedures are and follow them.

Other emergencies

During my career, I have had to deal with:

○ being attacked verbally across the classroom by an aggrieved mother who had managed to penetrate the school's security system and appeared to be becoming violent

○ a post-retirement colleague who was kicked to the ground and injured in the eye by two teenage intruders whom he confronted. I drove him to hospital

○ a pupil who fell from a rope in the gym and had to be taken to hospital in an ambulance while I acted *in loco parentis* until the parents arrived

○ a pupil whose mother had been shot dead in the street and needed very careful and sympathetic management in school, both at the time and afterwards

○ a pupil whose front teeth were knocked out in a fall and whom I accompanied to an emergency dentist

○ a colleague who fainted in assembly.

Emergencies are unpredictable by definition. It is important to:

○ keep calm

○ think first of the safety and welfare of the children in your care

○ know the school's procedures and follow them to the letter if they're applicable, although sometimes the agreed procedures don't readily match a completely unforeseen emergency

○ get help as quickly as possible.

The Curriculum

| **4** |

Compulsory subjects

Key Stage 3

- English
- Mathematics
- Science
- Design and technology (D&T)
- Information and communication technology (ICT)
- History
- Geography
- Modern foreign language(s)
- Art and design
- Music
- Physical education (PE)
- Religious education (RE)
- Personal, health and social education (PHSE) and citizenship
- Careers education.

Key Stage 4

- English
- Mathematics
- Science
- ICT
- Citizenship
- RE
- PE
- Sex education
- Careers education.

At Key Stage 4 there are also four 'entitlement subjects'. That means that schools must, by law, offer courses in these subjects for any pupil who wishes to study them.

- Arts
- D&T
- Humanities
- Modern foreign language(s).

Schools are also required to include work-related learning within the curriculum for all pupils at Key Stage 4. This involves learning about working practices, experiencing the work environment and developing skills for working life.

General teaching requirements in all subjects across Key Stages 3 and 4 are:

- inclusion
- use of language
- use of ICT
- health and safety.

LIST 21 Examinations and qualifications taken in secondary schools

○ Standard Assessment Tests (SATs): taken in English, mathematics and science at the end of Key Stage 3 by all pupils in state schools.

○ General Certificate of Secondary Education (GCSE): covers a wide range of subjects and can be taken at any age, but usually done at the end of Key Stage 4.

○ AS-level: may be done early (or late) but usually taken in three, four or five subjects at the end of Year 12.

○ A2-level: builds on AS-levels and usually taken in three or four subjects at the end of Year 13, before entry to higher education.

○ General National Vocational Qualification (GNVQ): cross-curricular, offering, for example, leisure and tourism or art and design, and taken at foundation or intermediate level (equivalent to two or four GCSEs respectively).

○ Advanced Vocational Certificate in Education (AVCE): builds on GNVQ, with courses equivalent to two A-levels in, for example, information and communications technology or health and social care.

○ National Vocational Qualification (NVQ): work-related, competence-based qualification at five levels, assessed by on-the-job observation and questioning. Used by some schools in partnership with local businesses.

○ International Baccalaureate (IB): challenging, post-16 diploma encompassing various subjects, a dissertation and community work. Accepted by higher education institutions as a respected alternative to AS/A2-levels.

○ Welsh Baccalaureate: overarching diploma currently (2005) being piloted in several Welsh schools.

○ Scottish Highers and Advanced Highers: standard 16+ and post-16 qualifications in Scotland.

Main examination boards

You will need to contact examination boards if, usually as head of department, you are trying to decide which syllabus to use for a GCSE (or other) course. Always compare all options before making a decision. Examination boards usually give helpful advice and are good at providing relevant continuing professional development.

- Qualifications and Curriculum Authority (QCA): 83 Piccadilly, London W1J 8QA. Tel: 020 7509 5555; Web: www.qca.org.uk; Email: info@qca.org.uk.
- Edexcel: One90 High Holborn, London WC1V 7BH. Tel: 0870 240 9800; Web: www.edexcel.org.uk.
- Oxford and Cambridge and Royal Society of Arts Examination Board (OCR): 1 Hills Road, Cambridge CB1 2EU. Tel: 01223 552552; Web: www.ocr.org.uk.
- Assessment and Qualifications Alliance (AQA): Devas Street, Manchester M15 6EX. Tel: 0161 953 1180; Web: www.aqa.org.uk; Email: mailbox@aqa.org.uk.
- Welsh Joint Education Committee (WJEC): 245 Western Avenue, Cardiff CF5 2YX. Tel: 029 2026 5000; Web: www.wjec.co.uk.
- Scottish Qualifications Authority (SQA): 24 Douglas Street, Glasgow G2 7NQ or Ironmills Road, Dalkeith, Midlothian EH22 1LE. Tel: 0845 279 1000; Web: www.sqa.org.uk; Email: customer@sqa.org.uk.
- City and Guilds: 1 Giltspur Street, London EC1A 9DD. Tel: 020 7294 2800; Web: www.cityandguilds.com; Email: enquiry@cityandguilds.com.

The timetable

The timetable is king in a secondary school. It dictates exactly what you will be doing, with whom and at precisely what hour of the day for an entire year. Until quite recently timetablers worked their alchemy with little flags on a huge board, like military strategists moving ships or troops. Today most schools use computer programs, but it always has to be refined by hand and there has never been a secondary school timetable in the history of education which didn't include some uncomfortable arrangements for some teachers – such as three challenging Year 9 classes one after another on a Friday afternoon.

Timetable variations include:

○ running a two-week system so that lessons are timetabled over a ten-day cycle instead of five
○ running a six- or seven-day system so that instead of being Wednesday it's Day 6, or whatever. This has the advantage that timetabled horrors become moveable feasts. That dreaded Friday afternoon may not be so bad when it falls on a Tuesday or Wednesday
○ having only four or five whole-hour slots each day instead of seven or eight shorter ones with the usual combinations of singles, doubles and trebles
○ not having simultaneous breaks but timetabling classes so that all breaks, including lunch, are staggered
○ serving breakfast at, say, 10am, with one or two lessons taught first
○ offering students a three-part day (morning, afternoon and early evening) for which staff teach only two sessions each day by working shifts
○ having one non-timetabled day a fortnight or month to create time for extension or enrichment activities and off-site visits
○ suspending the timetable for a whole week, perhaps termly or annually, to engage in whole-school themed work such as careers or drama week.

Post-16

The school-leaving age is 16 and compulsory education ends on an annually decreed date at the end of June. The majority of students, however, now remain in full-time education until they are 18 or 19 in:

○ the post-16 department or sixth form of a comprehensive or selective school
○ a sixth-form college
○ an FE college
○ other sorts or institution offering post-16 education, such as a special school.

Courses usually consist of:

○ AS-level
○ A2-level
○ additional GCSEs or GCSE retakes
○ GNVQ at foundation or intermediate level
○ Vocational Certificate of Education
○ NVQs
○ a combination of any of the above
○ International Baccalaureate.

Towards the end of the first year of post-16 education many students begin to look forward to starting higher education at the end of the second year. There is an interesting developmental role for teachers in:

○ advising students over choice of institution
○ advising students over choice of course/subject
○ visiting universities and networking with admissions tutors
○ advising students about personal statements on university admission (UCAS) forms
○ helping with mock interviews
○ rejoicing or commiserating and counselling when their university offers come in (or not)
○ being around when exam results arrive in August to help those who didn't get the required grades to meet their university offers.

LIST 25 Assessment

There are two main reasons for assessing pupils' work and progress:

○ to find out how they're getting on and help them with any problems you discover
○ for a formal/ public record of a pupil's achievement such as an exam result, a school report or rank order list.

Good teachers do both but are always aware of what they're assessing for at a particular time. 'Value added' is an accountancy term borrowed by education. It describes a pupil's improvement during several years in school over and above what he/she was expected to achieve in view of entry scores.

Assessment includes:

○ 'baseline' tests at the beginning of secondary school against which value added can later be measured
○ correcting pupils' written work and assigning a score or grade to it, usually in accordance with school or department policy
○ informal tests in class – written or oral – to assess what a pupil knows, has learned or can do
○ internal school examinations which are typically set in all main subjects at the end of each school year
○ SATs results at the end of Year 9
○ testing practical skills and recording achievements in, for example, PE
○ GCSE (and other) results which form part of a pupil's assessment profile before he/she embarks on post-16 work
○ writing reports for parents throughout school. All schools must do this annually, and many secondary schools do it more often
○ considering a pupil's achievement and potential when advising about university or post-school choices.

Careers, citizenship and PSHE

These three compulsory curriculum components are usually timetabled in most secondary schools, but they also have a habit of straying into all other lessons. You are doing your bit, whatever your subject, every time you find yourself touching on:

- relationships
- civil rights
- business
- recycling
- sex
- skills training
- voting
- smoking
- volunteering
- working with others
- pollution
- community
- healthy eating
- parenting
- drugs
- local government
- keeping fit through exercise
- central government
- the law
- the penal system
- taxation
- the court system
- travel to work
- alcohol
- job/HE applications.

Since such topics tend to come up at random, especially in, say, English lessons, they are in no particular order here!

Beyond the Compulsory Curriculum

 Music and drama

Many children (and adults) take examinations in music and drama which act as a measure of their progress and the standard they've achieved and are part of an extended curriculum. Key organizations, all of which provide extensive support for teachers, include:

- ❍ Associated Board of the Royal Schools of Music: 24 Portland Place, London W1B 1LU. Tel: 020 7636 5400; Web: www.abrsm.org.
  Individual examinations on a wide range of instruments from Grades 1–8. Also awards Music Medals which recognize and reward achievement of group-taught pupils from the early stages of learning an instrument.
- ❍ London Academy of Music and Dramatic Art (LAMDA): 155 Talgarth Road, London W14 9DA. Tel: 020 8834 0500; Web: www.lamda.org.uk; Email: exams@lamda.org.uk.
  Performance-based examinations in speech and drama for individuals and groups.
- ❍ Trinity College London: 89 Albert Embankment, London SE1 7TP. Tel: 020 7820 6100; Web: www.trinitycollege.co.uk; Email: info@trinitycollege.co.uk.
  Music examinations graded 1–8 and diplomas. Offers a wide range of speech and drama options for individuals, pairs and groups, including one on circus skills and another specifically on Shakespeare.
- ❍ English Speaking Board: 26a Princes Street, Southport PR8 1EQ. Tel: 01704 501730; Web: www.esbuk.org; Email: admin@esbuk.org.
  Various examinations in spoken English, conducted in a group setting.

L I S T 28   **Sport**

Young people need physical exercise for health, and there is a new drive to emphasize sport in schools (alongside healthier eating). Teachers, who need not be PE specialists, can do a lot to help. Sports which could be promoted by enthusiasts on the staff include:

- cricket
- tennis
- football
- rugby
- netball
- hockey
- athletics
- cycling
- table tennis
- swimming
- abseiling
- dance.

But, bear in mind that for many of these you will need extensive training and certification before you may supervise children doing them.

The PE department is often very glad of extra-department assistance with minority sports such as:

- rock climbing
- basketball
- badminton
- archery
- rowing.

You can also:

- spectate at as many school sports events as you can. It shows that you think sport matters
- take part in staff versus student matches.

Three more ways to develop yourself and your pupils

There are many tried and tested schemes established in schools – or waiting to be taken up – which complement the curriculum and help to develop the students as rounded individuals. They also offer wonderful opportunities to energetic teachers who lead them. Here are three of them:

○ Duke of Edinburgh's Award: Gulliver House, Madeira Walk, Windsor, Berkshire SL4 1EU. Tel: 01753 727400; Web: www.theaward.org; Email: info@theaward.org.
   Nearly 250,000 14–17-year-olds (7 per cent of the whole age range) are involved in work for bronze, silver or gold awards each year. They help the community, pursue a hobby, skill or interest, undertake PE, take part in expeditions and (for the gold award only) participate in a residential experience.

○ Young Enterprise UK: Peterley House, Peterley Road, Oxford OX4 2TZ. Tel: 01865 776845; Web: www.young-enterprise.org.uk; Email: info@young-enterprise.org.uk.
   A business and enterprise programme in which 150,000 young people start their own mini-businesses and learn how to manage them, supported by over 2,000 businesses.

○ BNA Blake Shield: PO Box 5682, Corby, Northamptonshire NN17 2ZW. Tel: 01536 262977; Web: www.bna-naturalists.org; Email: blakeshield@btopenworld.com.
   An annual environmental competition run by British Naturalists' Association for 11–16-year-olds who work with an adult team leader on projects involving plants, birds, insects and other animals. Work goes on throughout the year, although the competition deadline falls in July. Teacher-leaders can be (and often are) natural-history enthusiasts from all disciplines – not just the science department.

Pupils

6

LIST 30   Adolescents can be . . .

- Charming
- Keen
- Thoughtful
- Sensible
- Sensitive
- Good company
- Receptive
- Helpful
- Willing
- Enthusiastic
- Friendly
- Supportive
- Kind
- Hardworking
- Interested.

But they can also be:

- Truculent
- Dismissive
- Surly
- Difficult
- Challenging
- Ungracious
- Moody
- Capricious
- Uncooperative
- Critical
- Hostile
- Awkward
- Unpredictable
- Workshy.

The funny thing is that, quite often, they're almost all these at the same time. Put it down to hormones. Actually it's that very volatility which makes secondary school pupils such a challenge, but so delightful and satisfying to work with.

L I S T 31 Building a rapport

Teenagers will learn nothing from or with you unless you have a good working relationship with them based on mutual trust and respect.

○ Make sure you know everyone's name.
○ Talk to pupils as individuals as often as you can.
○ Engage pupils in conversation outside the classroom, e.g. in the dining area.
○ Make yourself friendly and approachable – but not a 'soft touch'.
○ Listen to what pupils say.
○ Try to remember personal facts about them, e.g. 'How's your Dad's broken leg now?'
○ Use humour but not sarcasm.
○ Cultivate a 'twinkle in the voice' so that you can register mild disapproval through tone but make it clear that it is not very serious, e.g. I often say 'You horrible child!' to someone who's forgotten a book.
○ Don't have favourites.
○ Be prepared to reveal yourself as a human being with occasional anecdotes about your life and family.
○ Show that you trust them.
○ Don't be afraid to cultivate 'lovable eccentricity'. Such teachers are often the most effective and memorable.

Managing behaviour

Sometimes pupils behave unacceptably – although probably not quite as often, fortunately, as some newspapers would have us believe. Many secondary schools have very clear discipline policies based on carefully specified courses of action and consequence. Follow these to the letter. If you're in a school where discipline is less structured, try this with your own classes:

○ Spend the first lesson of the year negotiating rules.
○ Get pupils – when they are still biddable in the first lesson – to suggest rules.
○ Write them on the board.
○ They will almost certainly come up with what you want:
  – no calling out
  – hands up to speak
  – no put-downs
  – reasonable noise levels
  – remembering to say please and thank you
  – no eating in lessons
  – putting equipment away at end of lessons, etc.
○ Print out a copy of these for each pupil and get them to sign it – they're unlikely to object. This is 'their' work.
○ Display the list in the classroom.
○ Be scrupulous about obeying the rules yourself.
○ From then on, if a rule is infringed a gentle reminder such as 'Please don't do that as it's against the rule we agreed on' stands a good chance of working. And the rest of the class will be on your side.

Helpful books about behaviour management:

○ *How to Manage Children's Challenging Behaviour* by Bill Rogers (ed.) (Paul Chapman)
○ *Cracking the Hard Class: strategies for managing the harder than average class* by Bill Rogers (Paul Chapman)
○ *Managing Behaviour in Classrooms* by John Visser (David Fulton)
○ *Behaviour in Schools: theory and practice for teachers* by Louise Porter (Open University Press)
○ *Getting the Buggers to Behave* by Sue Cowley (Continuum)

Pastoral needs

All secondary school pupils need structured help and guidance with:

- approaching school work
- balancing school, home and other interests
- making, maintaining and managing friendships in school
- growing up
- making school-related choices.

Many also turn to teachers for other, more difficult, reasons such as:

- parents separating
- parent or other close family member is seriously ill
- student is seriously ill
- death in the family or at school
- female student is pregnant
- male student's girlfriend is pregnant
- coping with the psychological after-effects of abortion
- parent is in prison
- parent is awaiting trial
- student is awaiting trial
- student is abused at home or elsewhere
- family members are in danger in other countries.

In most secondary schools there is a designated 'pastoral' person assigned to every pupil – typically the form tutor. Children have a habit, however, of deciding for themselves who they want to confide in. Be prepared to listen, but make it clear that you can never offer a pupil absolute confidentiality. Explain that you may have to seek advice or take the problem to someone with expertise to deal with it, but that you will, of course, keep the pupil fully involved.

L I S T 34   **Working with parents**

The stronger your relationship with their parents, the more effective pupil education is likely to be. Think of it as a three-way partnership between you, the pupil and the parent(s), and learn to cultivate those links.

- Support the work of the school's parent-teacher association (PTA), if there is one.
- Start a PTA if the school doesn't have one.
- Structure parents' consultation meetings so that parents get a real chance to talk about their children's progress in privacy.
- Encourage parents to make appointments to come into school at other times to discuss matters too complex to deal with quickly at routine consultation evenings.
- Use homework diaries or weekly record/planner books – these can be a line of communication with parents who are asked to sign them regularly.
- Attend the annual governors' meeting with parents.
- Invite parents into school to help as volunteers/mentors, etc.
- Tap into parents' professional expertise, such as the father who's a fire officer and may be willing to talk to your Year 8 citizenship group.
- Talk to parents about sponsorship. They often have useful community contacts.
- Make a point of chatting informally to parents when they attend events such as sports fixtures or concerts.

Twins, triplets and more

No one teaches for long without encountering twins. Many of us at some stage in a career also teach triplets or more.

Some facts

- One in every 67 pregnancies ended in a multiple birth in 2003 (the most recent year for which statistics are available at the time of writing).
- The rate has risen from one in a hundred pregnancies since 1982, mainly because of reproductive technology.
- Numbers of twin births are now levelling off.
- Triplet (and other multiple) births rose to a peak in 1998 but are now back to 1986 levels.
- More information from Twins and Multiple Births Association at www.tamba.org.uk.

In secondary school

- Always treat twins as individuals.
- If they're identical (most twins are not) find some way of telling them apart – allow two distinguishing colour badges with school uniforms or some other variant.
- Be scrupulous about using their names. Never address one as 'Twin . . .'
- Encourage other pupils always to respect twins' individuality.
- Consider, in consultation with parents, putting them in different forms, houses, classes and/or sets to allow individual development.
- Be sensitive to the fact that twins are often exceptionally close mentally and emotionally.
- Being a twin has pros and cons. Friendships and other relationships can get tricky during adolescence. Secondary school teachers should be alert to this.

LIST 36 Trips

Taking pupils out on school trips, whether residential or for a single day, can be one of the most rewarding things a teacher ever does because:

- ○ you see the pupils in another context
- ○ they see you in a different light
- ○ another environment can change the dynamic of the relationship between you and the pupils
- ○ it's a different teaching and learning experience
- ○ everyone (including the teacher) can learn together in a friendly way
- ○ staff on trips usually get to know the colleagues they're working with better
- ○ rapport formed on trips can be further developed back in school.

Secondary school trip opportunities

- ○ Subject-related visits such as a GCSE biology pond-dipping excursion.
- ○ Theatre visits in connection with English, drama, other subjects or general, free-for-all education.
- ○ Visits to other schools to take part in shared projects, e.g. careers education.
- ○ 'Pastoral' residential trips, such as a year group going on a residential outdoor education trip.
- ○ 'Away' sports fixtures.
- ○ Residential exchanges in, say, France, Germany or Spain for language development.
- ○ Sports tours abroad, such as the hockey team going to the USA.
- ○ General interest learning trip abroad, typically organized by an enthusiastic member of staff – not necessarily related to his/her own specialism.
- ○ Going out of school to work with, or for, a charity.
- ○ Taking plays and concerts out of school for performance elsewhere, e.g. to local primary schools.

LIST 37 · Varying your teaching style

People learn in many different ways. And if you are trying to hold the attention of volatile teenagers, every one of whom probably has his or her preferred way of learning, it is essential that you vary your teaching style as often as possible. Depending on your subject and the resources available your students could:

○ work in groups
○ work in pairs
○ work as individuals
○ use the Internet
○ take part in a class debate
○ devise a role-play
○ work in the school library
○ work from a textbook
○ listen to you
○ make up/or participate in a quiz
○ design a poster
○ invite in, and work with, an outside speaker
○ construct graphs or diagrams
○ prepare presentations for the rest of the group
○ write notes and essays
○ read silently in class
○ gather data from their own experiments
○ study documents.

Teaching the opposite sex

If you are a woman teaching adolescent boys or a man teaching girls there are pitfalls to be avoided, particularly in single-sex schools which routinely now have both men and women on the staff. Most potential problems are easily preventable: it's a case of awareness and common sense.

- ○ Never allow sexually orientated banter or over-familiarity, even as a joke. It can very easily get out of control.
- ○ Do not 'flirt' with pupils, however innocently – hormone-ridden teenagers might misread the signals.
- ○ Never wear suggestive clothing. A very short skirt on a long-legged teacher in her 20s, for example, could be too much for a 17-year-old boy.
- ○ Never work one-to-one in a closed room with a pupil of the opposite sex. Always leave the door ajar and make sure there is someone else around.
- ○ Send for a colleague of the opposite sex if a student of the opposite sex is taken ill in your lesson and requires physical help.
- ○ Be very careful about touch – even a sympathetic pat on the arm or back is probably best avoided.
- ○ Make the boundaries (in every sense) very clear.
- ○ If you're male, and a teenage girl or group of girls clearly has a 'crush' on you, get a female colleague to speak to her/them to nip the problem in the bud.
- ○ Similarly, if you're female, be vigilant. If necessary, seek help in dealing with boys who may be developing inappropriate feelings for you.

LIST 39 — Should you teach your own children?

Do you want your own children in the school you teach at or possibly even in your classes? There are advantages and disadvantages.

Advantages

- You know all your child's teachers well.
- You and you child have shared experience – which is good for bonding.
- If there is a problem at school you will probably pick it up quickly and then be on hand to deal with it.
- No pick-up or drop-off problem.
- No 'childcare' difficulties for your lower secondary children. If you have to stay late they can come and join you.
- If you drive him or her to school it saves travel costs.
- Most staff children quickly learn not to gossip at school or to repeat certain things they hear at home.

Disadvantages

- Neither you nor the child has the 'at work privacy' most of us enjoy away from our families.
- Colleagues may try to discuss your child with you more than they would with 'outside parents'.
- Staff children sometimes suffer 'negative favouritism'. Parents try so hard not to favour their own children that actually they discriminate against them.
- Teachers are sometime inhibited about teaching a colleague's child.
- You may not want your child's friends (also your pupils) in your home, which prevents your child having normal friendships.

Teachers who are proud of the schools they teach in often say, 'This is the best school in the district. I wouldn't want my child to go anywhere else', or, 'What sort of message would I give parents about this school if I appeared to have so little faith in it that I chose to send my own children elsewhere?'

Colleagues | 7

L I S T 40 Staffrooms

There are three sorts:

- recreational or rest area with comfortable seating and, often, refreshments
- work room with individual desks, shelves and sometimes even a computer terminal for each teacher
- administration area with pigeonholes, shared computers, phone, photocopier, etc.

Some schools, especially in the independent sector, offer all staff the use of all three. In many others, one multi-purpose room has to do.

New secondary schools are sometimes built without 'recreational' staff rooms – presumably because there's no rest or respite on offer. In such schools refreshments are served in a communal area with the students and there are small areas for administration or desk work.

A secondary school's staff is sometime known as The Staff Room (or Common Room) in the same way as magistrates are referred to as The Bench or police as The Law.

In a traditional staffroom

You might find:

○ mouldy, half-eaten sandwiches
○ dusty piles of last year's coursework
○ noticeboards
○ newspapers – old and today's
○ weary, broken-springed sofas and armchairs
○ defunct pencils and pens
○ unwashed, cracked coffee mugs
○ seats which newcomers are advised not to sit in because 'Bill likes to sit there. He's coming up to retirement and a bit moody, so ...'
○ half-completed marking which must be neither moved nor touched
○ banana skins
○ crisp packets
○ threadbare carpets
○ a hot water heater, often erratic and noisy, for tea and coffee
○ a fridge for milk and into which well-organized colleagues (there are a few in every school) put their packed lunches
○ cartoons and jokes pinned or stuck here and there by waggish colleagues
○ no pupils – with luck (but don't bank on it).

And, during breaks, you will hear conversation about:

○ what happened on *EastEnders* last night
○ the Government's latest threat to teachers' salaries, working conditions or status reported in today's copy of the *Guardian*
○ the latest report of pupil misbehaviour which is all over the front of today's *Daily Mail*
○ one hopeful colleague's pension predictions which have just been sent by Teachers' Pensions
○ the dreadful RE lesson a weak colleague has just endured with Year 9 in which Flossie Featherington was appallingly rude and incited the whole group to riot
○ this Saturday's big international match – tennis, football, rugby or whatever.

- the forthcoming wedding of a colleague's daughter and the complex preparations for it
- whether or not certain pupils may be released from your, or someone else's, lesson tomorrow because they are needed for music rehearsal, sports fixture or oral examination.

Staffroom reading matter

You can learn a great deal about the secret pleasures, pastimes and vices of secondary school teachers and the schools they work in from looking unobtrusively at the staffroom clutter to see what magazines and newspapers they read during snatched breaks. A teacher will usually look up for long enough to tell a visitor that he/she confiscated whatever it is from a pupil . . . Some of the titles, many of them old and well thumbed, I have seen in secondary school staffrooms include:

- The *Sun*
- *Angling Times*
- *Amateur Photographer*
- *Vogue*
- *Playboy*
- *Private Eye*
- *Good Housekeeping*
- *Cat World*
- *Conference and Common Room*
- The *TES*
- *Daily Mail*
- The *Guardian*
- *Country Life*
- *Report*
- The *Daily Telegraph*
- *Just 17*
- *The Times*
- *Viz*
- *Big Issue*
- *The Stage*
- *New Statesman*
- *National Trust Magazine*
- *The Independent*
- *The Oldie*
- *Hello!*
- The *Church Times*
- *Men's Health*
- *What Car?*
- *Opera Now*

Get to know the right people

If you're new in a secondary school there are certain key, non-teaching staff with whom you need to make friends – fast.

- ◯ Caretaker: he'll fix that window in your classroom which is stuck shut. It probably isn't really his (or her) job – but smile . . .
- ◯ Reprographics staff: if you're on good terms with them they might give your photocopying priority, even though you forgot to give it to them earlier.
- ◯ Catering staff: do you want some decent lunch saved when you know you're going to be late getting to the dining room?
- ◯ Your classroom cleaner: it's vital that he or she keeps your room wholesome. Chat to him/her. Say thank you regularly and maybe buy the odd small gift.
- ◯ The headteacher's PA: she or he is gatekeeper to your boss and you might need an appointment.
- ◯ Lab technician: if you teach science and you want your lessons to run smoothly with the right equipment, this is a key contact.

My car was once towed out of the mud on school premises by a kindly school caretaker. Would I still be there if I hadn't been pally with him?

Working in the same school as your spouse or partner

It happens – usually either because one of the partners knows there's an opening in his or her school and introduces, or tips off, the other, or because two people meet and 'become an item' in their mutual workplace.

The pros

○ Each of you understands the daily stresses of the other.

○ You can mull over school issues at home and sort them out supportively in private.

○ You probably both teach or know the school's most difficult/ ideal pupils and can get frustrations, etc., off your chests without involving anyone else.

○ You can travel in the same car and save fuel costs.

○ It's handy to pick up the week's groceries and or children/booze/ dry-cleaning together on your way home from school.

The cons

○ You can get very insular.

○ It can make problems if one of you is senior to, or has to line-manage, the other, especially if there's a 'capability' issue.

○ Presumed 'pillow talk' may stop colleagues sharing confidentialities with either of you.

○ If you're not careful you can find yourself earnestly discussing next year's timetable when lying on the beach at Marbella, cruising on the Nile or walking the Pennine Way.

LIST 45 Teaching colleagues' children

At some stage in your teaching life you may find that some of the pupils in your classes are the children of your colleagues.

○ Treat them exactly as you would any other pupils.
○ Avoid favouritism, positive or negative.
○ Commend and reprimand as freely as necessary.
○ Never mention the relationship in the classroom in front of the class. Play it down.
○ Refer problems and achievements to the form teacher or head of year in the usual way.
○ Involve the parent only if you would phone or write home if this parent weren't also a colleague.
○ Don't be daunted if the pupil is the child of a colleague who is very senior to you – perhaps even the headteacher.

I have often taught colleagues' children for some time before realizing who their parents were. This can happen quite easily in a largish school when the surname is common. One London deputy head insisted that his children use their mother's name (his wife hadn't taken his name) in school to blur his connection with them – not a bad idea.

Support staff

Support staff – those non-teachers who work in secondary schools, often in crucial and senior positions – now have a wide range of roles. The implementation of the workload agreement in September 2005 means that teachers now undertake fewer non-teaching tasks, so the number of jobs for adults in schools continues to grow. They include:

○ classroom assistant
○ learning assistant
○ higher learning assistant
○ bursar
○ school administrator
○ receptionist
○ school nurse
○ department administrator (in a big school a large department such as mathematics or English may have full- or part-time administrative support)
○ headteacher's PA
○ PA to other senior staff
○ drama technician
○ science technician
○ ICT technician
○ network manager
○ school secretary
○ midday meal supervisor
○ catering assistant
○ cook
○ restaurant manager
○ librarian
○ reprographics assistant
○ attendance/welfare manager.

Governors

A school's governing body is its highest level of management. It is directly responsible for appointing the headteacher, is involved in all senior appointments and takes responsibility for the ultimate management of money. Governors include LEA reps and, in the case of a specialist school, city technology college (CTC) or city academy, sponsors are represented too. Think of school governors as colleagues rather than as a threat. They, like you, are looking to do what's best for the school and its pupils and staff.

- Make sure you know the chairman's name and that you would recognize him or her.
- Take any opportunity you can to meet and talk to governors so that you get to know them.
- Be welcoming when they come into school during the day.
- Invite them to your lessons.
- Attend the governors' annual meeting with parents.
- Find out which governor is responsible for what, such as who chairs the finance sub-committee.
- Make sure you know the parent governors and establish a rapport with them.
- Make sure you know who the teacher governors are – they are your formal link with the governing body.
- Consider standing for election as a teacher governor in the next round of elections.

LIST 48 Colleagues and performance management

Some teachers find it difficult to accept appraisal by a colleague. Suddenly the head of department or line manager who has always been so encouraging and helpful seems to be sitting in judgement. And if you are the performance manager it can be a tricky role change to manage.

○ Approach performance management positively.
○ You are there to help others improve, or to be helped to do a better job yourself.
○ Remind yourself that all pupils (and they are, presumably, why you came into teaching) deserve to be taught by the best possible teachers.
○ Make performance management meetings business-like but friendly.
○ Hold them in an office (not the corner of the staffroom or anywhere you can be interrupted).
○ Be scrupulous about punctuality.
○ Take time to establish a courteous but relaxed atmosphere – you are not strangers. Look after each other.
○ Learn from your colleague – it's always a two-way process. The appraisee has something to give too.
○ Be thoughtful about paperwork, such as notes on the meeting – agree on the wording.
○ Allow as much time as such meetings need, don't try to rush through them.
○ Follow up the conclusions – such undergoing or organizing training – scrupulously.

The literary view

Writers, many of them poets, have always celebrated or condemned teachers, teaching and school life. These handy quotes might impress your colleagues at staff meetings.

○ *. . . a rotten day at school –*
Sweat on my fingers, pages thumbed with smears,
Cane smashing down to make me keep them neat
Philip Hobsbaum

○ *When will the bell ring, and end this weariness?*
How long have they tugged the leash and strained apart,
My pack of unruly hounds?
D.H. Lawrence

○ *What counts might not be countable. What can be counted might not count.*
Albert Einstein

○ *The village master taught his little school.*
A man severe he was and stern to view
Oliver Goldsmith

○ *He who can does. He who cannot teaches.*
George Bernard Shaw

○ *Then the whining schoolboy, with his satchel*
And shining morning face, creeping like snail
Unwillingly to school.
William Shakespeare

○ *It were better to perish than to continue schoolmastering*
Thomas Carlyle

○ *A child's mind is a fire to ignite and not a vessel to fill*
Attributed to various writers, including Tacitus.

Team Playing

L I S T 50 Role of the form tutor

A secondary school form tutor:

○ tries to pick up and follow on from the primary school teacher, especially with Year 7

○ should know every member of the form/tutor group well

○ is the first point of contact with the school for parents

○ marks the register

○ is pupils' first pastoral port of call

○ works with the form to bond friendships, etc.

○ may take or organize tutor group assemblies in his or her own classroom

○ may lead the form in devising an assembly for the year group or whole school

○ writes summary comments on reports for pupils in the tutor group once subject teachers have reported

○ may teach the form for cross-curricular subjects such as PSHE or citizenship

○ liaises between pupils in the tutor group and staff colleagues as and when necessary

○ may have a new form each year or may move up through the school with the same group.

LIST 51 Being part of a team of tutors

Secondary school form tutors need to work together to share:

○ expertise
○ good practice
○ policy decisions affecting all groups
○ practical, everyday information
○ administrative details
○ problems.

This usually means tutors meeting regularly in a group under a team leader, such as the head of year or pastoral team leader for Key Stage 4. Depending on the size, layout and organization of the school, the group could comprise all the form tutors in:

○ one year
○ one house (typically one or two forms from each year in each house)
○ one building (if, say, Years 7 and 8 are on one site and the rest of the school elsewhere)
○ Key Stage 3, Key Stage 4 or post-16.

Being a member of a department or faculty

Whatever your subject, in a secondary school you will be part of a department or faculty. If you teach two fairly discrete subjects such as mathematics and RE you may even find yourself with a foot in two (or more) departments. Sometimes if small school departments, such as music, consist of only one teacher, that isolated teacher becomes part of the humanities or arts faculty – this is why many schools now have larger faculties instead of the traditional departments.

Members of the department or faculty team:

○ have a common way of working
○ use similar programmes of study
○ are encouraged by Ofsted to have a department /faculty handbook
○ devise or buy and share resources
○ can cover for each other fairly easily
○ meet regularly to discuss curricular and administrative matters
○ must make collective decisions about the management of GCSE and post-16 course work
○ may sometimes team-teach
○ may share teaching space, such as a suite of classrooms
○ may have a designated administrative and staff work area within the school.

Middle management groups

If you are a head of department/faculty or a pastoral leader (head of year, house, etc.) you will have issues in common with others in school holding parallel posts. There will be meetings and other opportunities to share information and good practice – you are a member of another team!

○ Use your subject association for subject-specific management guidance (see List 6 Joining a subject association)
○ If yours is a pastoral post, join the National Association for Pastoral Care in Education. It publishes a journal, organizes conferences and disseminates guidance for its members. NAPCE, Institute of Education, University of Warwick, Coventry CV4 7AL. Tel: 024 765 23810; Web: www.warwick.ac.uk/wie/napce; Email: napce@napce.org.uk.
○ If you're new in post remember you can learn a lot from other, more experienced post holders. Listen to them and don't be afraid to ask for advice.
○ If you've been doing the job for some time you can probably help less experienced colleagues, but it's usually best to wait to be asked!
○ Remember that, like any team, an assembly of, say, heads of department is much stronger than the sum of its parts. Sharing concerns is often the best possible way of dealing with them.

LIST 54   Senior management or leadership group

In many schools management/leadership teams are much larger than they used to be. Although the headteacher or principal remains firmly at the top, the structure tends now to be more 'flat' than hierarchical. A secondary school senior management team (SMT) may now include:

- ○ headteacher or principal
- ○ several deputy heads or principals
- ○ several assistant heads or principals
- ○ bursar
- ○ heads of faculty
- ○ head's or principal's PA
- ○ manager of specialism, if it's a specialist school.

(Some of these roles may overlap.)

Useful contacts for senior managers

- ○ National Association of Head Teachers (NAHT): 1 Heath Square, Boltro Road, Haywards Heath, West Sussex RH16 1BL. Tel: 01444 472472; Web: www.naht.org.uk; Email: info@naht.org.uk.
- ○ Secondary Heads Association (SHA): 130 Regent Road, Leicester LE1 7PG. Tel: 0116 299 1122; Web: www.sha.org.uk; Email: info@sha.org.uk.
- ○ National College for School Leadership (NCSL): Triumph Road, Nottingham NG8 1DH. Tel: 0870 001 1155; Web: www.ncsl.org.uk; Email: ncsl-office@ncsl.org.uk.

LIST 55 Managing meetings

- Keep them as short as possible.
- Devise an agenda which puts things in order of importance.
- Ask colleagues in advance for items they would like to be included on the agenda.
- Don't hold a meeting for the sake of it – if there's nothing to discuss then cancel the weekly/monthly meeting.
- Find a way – humour may do the trick – of shutting up the person who likes lengthily to hold the floor on every topic at every meeting and makes everyone else sigh inwardly (or outwardly, depending on the time of day and the level of exasperation) whenever she or he draws breath to speak. There is one in every team.
- Find a way of drawing out and including the person who says very little. Have a quiet word outside the meeting to find out why.
- Don't hold meetings about meetings.
- End meetings punctually.
- Provide little treats, such as chocolate biscuits or a glass of wine, to help get things going in an affable way.
- Don't allow yourself to be intimidated by the presence of staff that are, in other school contexts, senior to you. (For example, you are head of geography, but the headteacher happens also to be a geographer and teaches one GCSE class so she attends your meetings as a member of the department. *You* are chairing this meeting.)

Supporting colleagues

The entire school staff is a team, from the headteacher to the most junior trainee in the kitchen. Team members should all help and support each other. Some guidelines:

○ If a colleague is reprimanding a truculent pupil it can help simply to stand nearby. Solidarity is a powerful tool.

○ Never gossip to students about colleagues or pass on anything personal without the colleague's express permission (for example, Mrs Smith is going on maternity leave at the end of this term or Mr Jones is retiring next year).

○ If a student complains to you about a colleague's unfair/ unacceptable/incompetent behaviour or attitude, listen but don't comment. Tell the student you will make enquiries. You may need to involve the headteacher and/or talk to the colleague, depending on the circumstances.

○ Talk to students positively about colleagues. 'Why don't you ask Mr James about that? I don't know the answer but he's hugely knowledgeable about the Tudor period.'

○ Never criticize a colleague to, or in front of, students.

○ Always put the needs and interest of a pupil before those of a colleague. That is your 'duty of care' (for example, if a colleague and friend is drunk in school you must report it. Pupils could be at risk and that must come before your personal loyalty to the colleague).

Other school teams

All secondary schools have working parties, committees, panels and groups in which staff work together in teams. For example, you might be part of the:

- ○ staff social committee
- ○ dinner-queue working party
- ○ school uniform panel
- ○ off-site trips advisory group
- ○ school meals committee
- ○ PSHE panel
- ○ assemblies committee
- ○ car park working party
- ○ fundraising committee
- ○ charities liaison group
- ○ library committee
- ○ headteacher's advisory panel.

Whatever your subject, there are also plenty of extra-curricular teams for you to join in a big secondary school. You might make yourself part of the:

- ○ school choir
- ○ staff cricket team
- ○ school orchestra
- ○ staff jazz band
- ○ cast of a staff play
- ○ cast of the school play
- ○ technical team doing lighting or sound for a school production
- ○ staff quiz team
- ○ school band
- ○ staff netball/rounders/football/ hockey team (which typically plays a student team and loses ignominiously)
- ○ sponsored walk, run or swim relay team for charity.

General Teaching Council (GTC)

All teachers employed in the maintained sector ('state schools') in England and Wales have to be registered with either the GTCE (England) or the GTCW (Wales). Think of it as being part of a nationwide team.

○ GTCE: Whittington House, 19–30 Albert Place, London WC1E 7EA and Victoria Square House, Victoria Square, Birmingham B2 4AJ. Tel: 0870 001 0308; Web: www.gtce.org.uk; Email: info@gtce.org.uk.

○ GTCW: 4th Floor, Southgate House, Wood Street, Cardiff CF10 1EW. Tel: 029 2055 0350; Web: www.gtcw.org.uk; Email: information@gtcw.org.uk.

○ The Council's main role is disciplinary decision-making about teachers' alleged professional misconduct.

○ Various publications include:
   – *Teaching* (England. Termly magazine, also available online)
   – *Teaching Wales* (Wales. Termly magazine, also available online)
   – *Connect* (England. Termly electronic newsletter about professional development)
   – *Achieve* (England. Magazine about racial equality, also available online).

○ Both councils have a strong events and conference programme.

○ Regional meetings enable teachers to meet GTC personnel and to take part in discussions.

○ Research by teachers and of interest to teachers is regularly published on the GTCE website.

○ There is a growing commitment to CPD (continuing professional development) at both GTCE and GTCW.

○ Registration fees (2005/6) are £30 a year in England and £32 in Wales. Staff working for LEAs (not supply teachers) are paid an annual grant of £33 to cover the fee.

Continuing Professional Development

Whole school INSET

INSET, or in-service training, mostly takes place on designated days when the pupils are absent, usually five times a year. Training may consist of:

○ presentation by an outside speaker on a topic of interest to the whole staff, e.g. health and safety, usually with activities, etc.
○ training led for the whole staff by one or more of the school's own staff, e.g. gifted and talented coordinator
○ development work such as curriculum planning undertaken in departments or other groups
○ joining with another school or schools to share a prestigious (i.e. costly!) speaker or presenter.

Disadvantages

○ It is rare for everyone on a staff to have identical training needs, so the chosen INSET is unlikely to be suitable for everyone.
○ Staff, understandably, can get resentful at wasted time if a speaker is sub-standard or the content is unsuitable.
○ It can seem expensive.
○ Some teachers feel it isn't 'proper' training if they've only sat in their own school hall – it is sometimes considered to lack the prestige of an 'off-site' course.

Advantages

○ Research shows that teachers' learning is more effective if a group of colleagues has collaborated and can implement it together afterwards.

○ The cost of the speaker can be quite modest if the fee is regarded as shared by the whole staff (e.g. £500 fee, 100 staff, therefore only £5 per head from the CPD budget).

L I S T 60   External courses

LEAs and examination boards run a lot of courses on pastoral, management, academic and whole-school issues for secondary teachers. So do course providers such as:

○ ChristopherSwann.com Professional Development: Suite 408–10, The Corn Exchange, Fenwick Street, Liverpool L2 7QS. Tel: 0845 125 9010; Web: www.christopherswann.com; Email:info@christopherswann.com.
○ Mill Wharf Training and Consultancy Services: Mill Wharf, Mill Street, Birmingham B6 4BU. Tel: 0121 628 2910; Web: www.mill-wharf-training.co.uk; Email: information@mill-wharf-training.co.uk.
○ Creative Education: 89 Sanderstead Road, South Croydon, Surrey CR2 0PF. Tel: 020 8666 0234; Web: www.creativeeducation.co.uk; Email: courses@creativeeducation.co.uk.
○ SfE Ltd: 1 Portland Square, Bristol BS2 8RR. Tel: 0117 983 8800; Web: www.sfe.co.uk; Email: mail@sfe.co.uk.
○ Network Training: Mitre House, Tower Street, Taunton, Somerset TA1 4BH. Tel: 01823 353354; Web: www.network-training.ac.uk; Email: mail@network-training.ac.uk.

L I S T 61   Distance learning

Many teachers now choose to improve their skills and/or
qualifications through distance learning. There are many
postgraduate courses which can be studied through online teaching,
occasional weekend or holiday face-to-face tutorials and tutor-
marked assignments returned electronically or by post.
Qualifications include:

- ○ MA (Master of Arts)
- ○ MBA (Master of Business Administration)
- ○ MEd (Master of Education)
- ○ MSc (Master of Science)
- ○ PhD or DPhil (Doctor of Philosophy)
- ○ EdD (Doctor of Education)

Modules leading towards these degrees can often be taken as stand-
alones and/or counted towards various certificates and diplomas.
Many universities and institutes of education now have a distance
learning arm. The highly respected Open University pioneered
distance learning and is a good starting point if you are considering
this way of studying: The Open University, Walton Hall, Milton
Keynes MK7 6AA. Tel: 01908 274066; Web: www.open.ac.uk.

L I S T 62   Mentoring and coaching

Mentoring someone means giving advice from your own experience. Coaching a colleague means – as it does in, say, football – looking closely at someone's performance and encouraging improvement in every possible way. It is a valuable form of CPD to be involved in mentoring or coaching. Both colleagues learn.

A secondary teacher being coached or mentored gets:

○ advice
○ someone to bounce ideas off
○ impartial comment
○ a focus on details which might otherwise go unnoticed
○ opportunities to discuss the quality of his or her work in a professional way.

A mentor or coach gets:

○ insights into a colleague's work
○ opportunities to analyse and reflect on what makes good practice
○ the challenge of coming up with workable suggestions to help a colleague
○ the chance to consider his or her own work afresh by comparing it with a colleague's
○ time set aside for professional discussion and debate.

LIST 63 Peer classroom observation

Team up with a trusted colleague. Observe each other's lessons and then feed back afterwards in an impartial, professional way. This is an invaluable form of CPD, especially if you teach different subjects. Things to look at closely include:

- beginning of lesson
- end of lesson
- how much opportunity pupils are given to interact
- pacing of lesson
- handling of resources
- management of pupil behaviour
- preparation of material in advance
- teacher's body language
- teacher's use of language to pupils
- teacher's rapport with pupils (use of names, thanking them for contributions, etc.)
- level of engagement of pupils with the content of lesson
- handling of disciplinary infringements.

Sabbaticals

No, that isn't a joke. Some lucky teachers really do get paid time away from the classroom for:

○ teacher exchange (usually abroad)
○ research
○ to benefit from a scholarship
○ career break
○ study.

Opportunities

○ Some independent schools such as Benenden and Eton give teachers a paid sabbatical term off, by negotiation, every ten years.
○ HTI arranges and funds school leader placements in business – Tel: 024 7641 0104 Web: www.hti.org.uk.
○ The Goldsmiths Company offers grants for innovative projects (such a teacher going to New Zealand to study Maori culture) – Tel: 020 7606 7010; Web: www.thegoldsmiths.co.uk/education/refreshgrant.htm.
○ Gatsby Teacher Fellowships pays for teachers of mathematics, design and technology or science to undertake research – Tel: 020 7410 7127; Web: www.gtf.org.uk.
○ NUT funds a handful of CPD scholarships each year – Web: www.teachers.org.uk.
○ Some Oxford and Cambridge colleges offer one-term fellowships for teachers, but you have to ring round individual colleges to find out what's available.

LIST 65 International professional development

Working with colleagues in other countries benefits your own teaching and it might get you a trip to, say, Russia, Australia or Hong Kong. Teachers' international professional development (TIPD) is always regarded as a two-way process – all the teachers involved learn from each other. It can take several different forms.

- Organizing pupil exchanges with schools in other countries. This is mostly done in modern languages departments. Pupils and staff usually stay in the homes of students and teachers from the other school.
- Teacher exchange. You teach abroad for a term or a year while the teacher you're replacing works in your school in Britain. Sometimes exchangers use each other's homes and cars too. See www.britishcouncil.org/learning-ie-teaching-exchange.htm
- Short trips funded through the Government's TIPD scheme are managed by the Specialist Schools and Academies Trust (www.specialistschoolstrust.org.uk/tipd), British Council (www.britishcouncil.org/tipd), League of Exchange of Commonwealth Teachers (www.lect.org.uk) and Best Practice Network (www.bestpracticenet.co.uk).
- Taking time out to work in schools abroad through Voluntary Service Overseas (VSO) which requires teachers prepared to learn by giving their skills, usually for two years, in areas in need (www.vso.org.uk).
- Spending one summer holiday working in a school in South Africa, Ghana or Uganda through Link Community Development's Global Teachers Programme (www.lcd.org.uk).
- Video-conferencing with schools and teachers in other countries and setting up email links – the twenty-first century's answer to 'pen pals'!

Some schemes are for individuals, others are thematic and are for groups. For example, some teachers from Gloucestershire LEA went to Hungary in 2002 to study alternative ways of handling vocational education and, in 2004, a group from London Borough of Greenwich visited Texas to learn about behaviour management.

LIST 66 Keeping up to date

Keeping abreast of changes, developments and trends in education is part of your CPD.

Useful publications

- Education sections of national newspapers, especially the *Guardian* and the *Independent* which both publish weekly education supplements.
- *The TES* (*Times Education Supplement*).
- *The TSES* (*Times Scottish Education Supplement*).
- *The THES* (*Times Higher Education Supplement*).
- Magazines and newsletters produced by professional associations, e.g. NUT's *The Teacher*, ATL's *Report* or NAHT's *Leadership Focus*.
- Subject association journals, such as *British Journal of Teaching Physical Education* (www.pea.uk.com) or *Teaching History* (www.history.org.uk).
- *SecEd*, weekly (term time only) free newspaper published by MA Education and sent to every secondary school (including independents) in Britain (www.sec-ed.co.uk).
- Optimus' monthly newletters. More than 12 subscription-only titles including *Education Law Update* and *Secondary Headship* (www.optimuspub.co.uk).
- Questions Publishing's subscription-only magazines including *Managing Schools* and *Teaching Citizenship* (www.education-quest.com).

And don't forget the wealth of education updates now available online – there are far too many to list. Just browse!

LIST 67 School-based research

Undertaking research in your own school or area is regarded as one of the best ways of enhancing your CPD and adding to the general body of knowledge about teaching and learning.

Contacts

- GTC (England) publishes 'Research of the Month' on its website – Web: www.gtce.org.uk.
- Any higher education institution. There is a research component in all higher degrees on education subjects.
- British Educational Research Association (BERA) – Web: www.bera.ac.uk.
- National Foundation for Educational Research (NFER) – Web: www.nfer.ac.uk.
- TDA (Training and Development Agency for Schools, formerly Teacher Training Agency) has an expanded remit for CPD including the promotion of research, particularly through its school-based research consortia initiative – Web: www.tda.gov.uk.
- Evidence-Based Education UK – Web: www.cemcentre.org/ebeuk.
- Your LEA may have details of local research projects or teachers wishing to start them, with whom you might collaborate.

L I S T 68   CPD portfolios

If you've done it, value it. Keep an ongoing record of all aspects of your CPD. Do it electronically or simply put it in a ringbinder. Not only will it enhance your self-esteem, it could be used for performance management or in job interviews. Include in your portfolio:

- ○ degree and other certificates
- ○ attendance certificates for courses
- ○ notes on courses
- ○ record of mentoring or being mentored
- ○ record of coaching or being coached
- ○ classroom observation notes
- ○ research undertaken
- ○ visual evidence (photographs, film, etc.) of projects
- ○ samples of student work, if relevant
- ○ record of reading – books, etc. – on education topics
- ○ any other evidence of your learning.

Prune and update your portfolio regularly. New activities and achievements should continually supersede and supplant work done longer ago.

Five easy ways of learning to be a better teacher

○ Discuss teaching and learning with your students. They know better than anyone what works and what doesn't.

○ Ask yourself at the end of each day what you could have done better and resolve to do it differently next time.

○ Learn from yourself. Be aware of what you've done well each day and make sure that you repeat and build on it.

○ Listen to and watch more experienced colleagues around the building, with students, in assembly, in the dining area, outside, as well as inside their classrooms if you get the chance.

○ Read a book a month about teaching or about your specialist subject.

Books every teacher should have read

Read any good books lately? No, not those stern, academic books. We're talking entertainment here. Teachers are allowed to enjoy themselves, you know. These books are about teachers and teaching. Try them for inspiration, empathy or laughter.

- *To Sir, with Love* by E.R. Braithwaite. Black teacher tames teenagers in a challenging post-war East End school.
- *The Prime of Miss Jean Brodie* by Muriel Spark. Charismatic Scottish role model weaves magic for teenage girls in an academy.
- *The Learning Game: A Teacher's Inspirational Story* by Jonathan Smith. English teacher reflects on classroom life.
- *Over Hill and Dale* by Gervase Phinn. Hilarious anecdotes of a Yorkshire school inspector. First of a series.
- *A Wedding Man is Nicer than Cats, Miss* by Rachel Scott. Bradford teacher meets first wave of immigrant children in pre-multicultural 1950s.
- *The History Boys* by Alan Bennett. Play about education and its purpose premiered at the National Theatre in 2004 before touring the country. Funny, perceptive text published by Faber.

Each of these hugely enjoyable classics has a major education theme – still thought-provoking:

- *Hard Times* by Charles Dickens
- *Jane Eyre* by Charlotte Brontë
- *Sons and Lovers* by D.H. Lawrence
- *Cider with Rosie* by Laurie Lee.

What Type of School? 10

The infinite variety of schools

Applying for a job? Make sure you know what sort of school you're applying to. There's no such thing as a simple secondary school. It can be:

- for pupils aged 11–16
- for pupils aged 11–19
- for 14–19-year-olds only
- for post-16s (sixth-form college)
- single-sex
- mixed-sex
- specialist in a single specialism (e.g. technology)
- specialist in more than one specialism (e.g. science and music)
- non-specialist
- academically selective ('grammar')
- non-selective
- community
- foundation
- voluntary-aided (e.g. Church of England)
- voluntary-controlled (e.g. Roman Catholic)
- independent
- boarding
- day
- small (fewer than 400 pupils)
- large (more than 2,000 pupils)
- LEA special (catering for SEN pupils)
- special, run by a charity (e.g. National Autistic Society).

And most of these are not self-contained – the same school can fall into several categories.

LIST 72 Who pays?

Many secondary schools are part of the LEA's provision for the area, but many are also linked with other bodies in various ways and some are completely independent.

- Community schools (about half of all secondary schools in England and Wales) are owned and funded by their LEAs.
- Voluntary-controlled schools may have a religious ethos and the voluntary body may own the fabric, but the LEA bears all the costs.
- Voluntary-aided schools may also be housed in buildings owned by the voluntary body, although 90 per cent of the maintenance and improvement costs can be recouped from the LEA.
- Foundation schools are usually secular. They are funded by the LEA but their buildings are owned by the governors or by a foundation.
- There are 15 city technology colleges (CTCs) and these are essentially non-fee paying, independent schools within the state system. Most of them opened in the early 1990s. Sponsorship money helped to build them, and representatives of the sponsors sit on their governing bodies.
- City academies, usually referred to now simply as 'academies', are a newer version of CTCs.
- Independent schools charge fees. They are non-profit-making organizations and many have foundations which provide bursaries and scholarships to assist families in need. Christ's Hospital in Horsham, West Sussex, is the wealthiest, which is why it funds or part-funds many pupils.
- Private schools are the private businesses of their owners. They charge fees with the intention of making a profit.

L I S T 73   Selective or comprehensive?

Yes, selective or 'grammar' schools still exist within the state system in England, which sometimes comes as a surprise to people working or living in areas which have a fully comprehensive system. These can be found in:

- ○ Kent (the majority)
- ○ Lincolnshire
- ○ Buckinghamshire
- ○ Essex
- ○ The Midlands
- ○ some outer London boroughs.

Many LEAs have just one or two selective schools functioning alongside comprehensive schools.

Take care with terminology. The term 'grammar school' can be misleading because:

- ○ some former grammar schools (e.g. Steyning Grammar School in West Sussex) retain the title for historical reasons but are now comprehensive schools
- ○ some former grammar schools (e.g. Manchester Grammar School) are now fee-paying independent schools
- ○ some LEA selective schools (e.g. The Folkestone School for Girls) do not have 'grammar' in their name.

Specialist schools

The specialist schools movement began in 1994. More specialisms have gradually been introduced, and now nearly all secondary schools have specialist status.

A school wanting to specialize must:

- raise £50,000 in sponsorship (reduced from £100,000 in 1999)
- prepare a detailed application.
- They then get:
  - £100,000 capital grant (to add to the £50,000 sponsorship)
  - additional annual funding per pupil for four years.

Among other functions, the Specialist Schools and Academies Trust:

- supports schools in raising sponsorship and working with sponsors
- advises schools preparing applications for specialist status
- helps schools in its network to make the most of specialist status once it is granted.

Specialist Schools and Academies Trust: 16th Floor, Millbank Tower, 21–4 Millbank, London SW1P 4QP. Tel: 020 7802 2300; Web: www.specialistschools.org.uk; Email: info@specialistschools.org.uk.

Secondary schools seeking specialist status can choose from ten specialisms:

- Arts (performing or visual or media)
- Business and enterprise
- Engineering
- Humanities
- Languages
- Mathematics and computing
- Music
- Science
- Sports
- Technology.

Since 2003, combined specialisms have been allowed. These include:

○ Media arts + business and enterprise
○ Mathematics and computing + science
○ Performing arts + technology
○ Languages + humanities.

LIST 75   Single-sex or mixed?

○ There are fewer single-sex schools in Britain than there used to be. Many former girls' schools have merged with a nearby boys' school, often to form a single 'community college', but several hundred single-sex schools remain and most LEAs have some.

○ Many independent schools which were formerly for boys now take girls, either throughout the school or just at post-16.

○ Some single-sex grammar schools take both sexes at post-16.

○ Almost all single-sex schools now have a mixture of male and female staff.

○ If you have your eye on promotion outside your own school, try not to limit your experience to single-sex teaching.

Advantages of single-sex schools

○ Girls tend to do better academically in a single-sex environment.

○ Girls are often more confident if they have to take all the responsibility because there are no boys in the school.

○ Adolescent boys are often more focused and committed to work if they are not busy showing off to girls.

○ Some teachers are more comfortable teaching one sex or the other.

Advantages of mixed schools

○ Working with both sexes is good for staff development.

○ Adolescent girls and boys learn to develop cross-sex friendships without sexual involvements.

○ A mixed school is more 'natural' because the rest of the world consists of both males and females.

○ Some mixed schools teach pupils in single-sex groups to give them the best of all possible worlds!

Teaching in an independent school

- ○ Independent schools are not required to teach the National Curriculum, so lower secondary syllabuses may be more imaginative and possibly more rigorous.
- ○ Most (although not all) still enter pupils for GCSE, so the curriculum tends to become more 'mainstream' at Key Stage 4.
- ○ Fees are typically £20,000 or more per year for a boarding place in a famous school such as Winchester or Benenden.
- ○ Day places at secondary level range from about £6,000 to £12,000 per year.
- ○ Many independent schools offer fee concessions for the children of staff who teach there.
- ○ Most independent boarding schools offer accommodation for staff and their families.
- ○ Teaching hours in boarding schools are typically longer than those in day schools. 9am–5pm plus Saturday morning is not unusual.
- ○ Holidays are usually longer, which offsets the longer contact time during the term.
- ○ Independent schools usually offer a wide range of opportunities for staff to develop extra-curricular activities in, for example, sport, music and drama.
- ○ Most independent schools work with Teachers' Pensions so that service continues to count towards your pension – but check this with any school you are considering working in.
- ○ Teachers in independent schools are not required to register with the General Teaching Council (ETCE or ETCW), although many do.
- ○ The law does not require teachers in independent schools to hold Qualified Teacher Status (QTS), although most do.

State boarding schools

There are 35 schools in England which take boarders but which are part of the state education system, such as:

○ Royal Alexandra and Albert School, Surrey
○ Wymondham College, Norfolk
○ Dallam School, Cumbria.

The facts

○ Tuition is free but there are boarding costs.
○ Boarding fees average £9,000 per year.
○ Each school is part of the mainstream provision in the LEA in which it is situated, although boarders often come from other areas.
○ Most schools are mixed but there is a small number of single-sex schools.
○ Some schools have charitable foundations to help families in need.
○ Employers (e.g. armed forces) may help with boarding costs for parents whose work involves frequent moves or being abroad.
○ Teachers and their families are often accommodated within the school.
○ State Boarding Schools' Association: 35–7 Grosvenor Gardens, London SW1W OBS. Tel: 020 7798 1580; Web: www.sbsa.org.uk.

A new city academy, due to open in the London Borough of Southwark in 2008, plans to take some boarders. Residential fees will be paid by a sponsor. This is the first new state boarding school to open in 40 years and may be the beginning of a new trend, especially for pupils in need of extra stability in their lives.

LIST 78 Special schools

- Secondary education for children with physical, emotional, behavioural or ability-related special needs often takes place in a larger all-age school.
- Many special schools are run by LEAs.
- Some are run by charities as independent schools.
- LEAs 'buy' places for children in these schools if there is no other suitable provision within the area.
- Sometimes children come from other LEAs which are a long way away.
- Some pupils board at school, at least during the week.
- Most teachers employed in these schools are specially trained to work with the disability in question.

Charities running special schools across Britain include:

- Royal National Institute for the Blind: Web: www.rnib.org.uk.
- Shaftesbury Society (for pupils with multiple disabilities): Web: www.shaftesburysoc.org.uk.
- Scope (for pupils with cerebral palsy): Web: www.scope.org.uk.
- National Autistic Society: Web: www.nas.org.uk.
- Caldecott Foundation (for pupils with SEN 'arising out of unhappy and disturbed backgrounds'): Web: www.caldecottfoundation.co.uk.

Writing Documents | 11

Pupil reports: what not to say

When writing your reports on pupils, it's now customary to be positive and constructive – and to back your statements with evidence. The terse comments which your teachers may – a generation or two ago – have had fun writing about you, are no longer acceptable!

- Could do better if he tried.
- Carelessly spoils everything she does.
- Would do better if he attended more lessons.
- I don't know which is worse: her behaviour or her work.
- No improvement since the last report.
- Finds this subject difficult.
- Does he own a dictionary?
- The more she talks the less she achieves.
- This boy will get nowhere.
- I can't remember when I last saw any work from her.
- Distracts others.
- Shows no interest in this subject.
- Deserves all she gets.
- Bone idle.
- He is bound to fail the exam.

Pupil reports: what you can say

Here are just a few useful comments for constructive twenty-first century pupil reports.

- A good term's work for Jake, which culminated in an excellent essay/project/model/exam result.
- Marie's understanding of French verbs has really improved, as she showed in her recent role-play.
- Hamil has been a supportive member of the tutor group this term, particularly during the difficult time when the tutor room was being redecorated.
- I find Emma a hard-working and interested student.
- Ishmael is a pleasure to teach.
- Although I think Henry finds maths quite difficult he has worked hard and made real progress, as his recent test result shows.
- I hope Ella will go on working hard to build on the pleasing progress she has made this term.
- Olivia's contributions to discussions have helped everyone in the group.
- Gary's excellent exam result is well deserved.
- Now that Lewis has mastered the basics of algebra he needs to concentrate on geometry next term.

Emphasize the positives! Some handy 'report' words to apply to weak students you need to encourage include:

- pleasing
- cooperative
- willing
- enthusiastic
- conscientious
- thoughtful
- committed.

LIST 81   Reports and memos for colleagues

You might write internally to a colleague if, for example:

○ you have been on a course and a summary of its content needs sharing
○ a pupil has a medical or personal problem which colleagues need to know about. This would normally be confidential to the teachers involved
○ a form tutor requests an internal report on a student
○ the conclusions or findings of a school working party or committee need to be disseminated
○ you want feedback on a draft of any school document you are preparing
○ you need to inform colleagues about practical arrangements, such as room changes
○ you want to request a favour, such as the release of a student from a colleague's lesson to complete coursework in your subject.

Communications to colleagues should be:

○ polite
○ clear
○ succinct
○ accurate
○ relevant.

LIST 82 Department handbooks

It is good practice for every secondary school department to write and maintain a handbook. This ensures that everyone in the department knows how things are organized, and Ofsted inspectors may find it useful during inspection.

What to include

○ Names and job titles of all staff in the department.
○ Staff email addresses and telephone extensions.
○ Job descriptions for each member of the department, including support staff.
○ Each teacher's and teaching assistant's current timetable.
○ Key Stage 3 syllabus.
○ Outline information about GCSE and other courses (e.g. GNVQ) taught by the department at Key Stage 4, obtained from relevant examination boards, with guidance on where to find further information.
○ Outline information about AS, A2, VCE, GNVQ, IB and any other course taught at post-16, obtained from relevant examination boards, with guidance on where to find further information.
○ A guide to finding resources within the department – what is kept in which cupboard, filing cabinet or how to find it on the intranet.
○ Department policies on, for example, issuing books to students or dealing with coursework handed in late.
○ Specific health and safety policies in departments such as design and technology and PE.
○ Anything else which everyone in the department – especially an NQT or newcomer to the school – should know.

School policies

Nearly everything a school does, or which might ever happen to it, is now usually enshrined in written policy. These are written by teachers, sometimes in collaboration with governors. Look at policy-writing positively and regard it as a staff development opportunity. Policy-writing opportunities in secondary schools include:

- health and safety
- sex education
- child protection
- anti-bullying
- school visits
- inclusion
- discipline
- complaints
- illness in school
- intruders
- admissions
- staff absence
- lesson cover
- CPD
- dealing with the press.

LIST 84   **Writing to parents**

You might write and send to parents:

○ invitations to consultation meetings
○ individual letters about their son or daughter expressing concern about behaviour or some other issue
○ individual – but probably standardized – letters commending the pupil for good work or behaviour
○ information about a forthcoming school trip/play/event
○ a plea for help with a school event, such as asking for volunteers to man the car park or help with refreshments
○ a plea for items such as props for a school play or saleable goods for fundraising events
○ fundraising appeals
○ newsletters about activities, events and achievements in school.

Any of the above can be, and often are, sent by email these days, provided families have Internet access. It's cheaper and faster than ordinary mail and more likely to reach its destination than scruffy bits of 'pupil post' which often end their days at the bottom of bags and pockets.

L I S T 85   Risk assessments

Any school activity, especially an off-site trip, must be preceded by the preparation of a written risk assessment document. Some LEAs produce generic ones which can be adapted, and schools often have a proforma for frequent activities such as theatre trips, 'away' sports fixtures or biology field trips. The idea is to identify every potential risk so that you can ensure all possible steps are taken to avoid them.

○ A risk assessment can be defined as a careful examination of how people may be harmed from a particular activity or situation.
○ The assessment should then help you to see whether the risk can be reduced to a reasonable level through the introduction of control measures.
○ A 'hazard' is something with the potential to cause harm (e.g. a wet floor).
○ The document must by law show that:
  – a proper check has been made
  – all significant hazards have been dealt with, taking account of all the people who will be involved
  – the precautions are now reasonable and the remaining risk is low.
○ There are three main sorts of risk assessment document relating to off-site trips:
  – generic (e.g. to cover any coach journey)
  – group and site-specific (such as a visit to a specific venue, e.g. Caernarvon Castle)
  – ongoing (judgements are adjusted during a visit according to circumstances, e.g. changing weather).
○ More information at www.teachernet.gov.uk/management/atoz/r/riskmanagement.
○ Profomas may help. Try *Risk Assessment Documents for Secondary Schools* by Tony Attwood (2004) ISBN 1860837115. Published by First and Best in Education £25.95. 50 copiable sheets. Also on CD-ROM.

The school prospectus

The prospectus, which is sent out to prospective parents, is half the school's shop window (its other half is its website – see List 87). Its purpose is to persuade families with children in Year 6 to apply for secondary places at your school, so it has to look good and read well.

○ Use as many colour photographs as you can afford showing cheerful pupils learning (music, sport and drama lessons are especially photogenic).
○ Include a photograph of the headteacher looking friendly and working with students.
○ Describe the school's ethos.
○ Make it clear that this is a caring school which nurtures individuals.
○ Include some school history if it's applicable.
○ Summarize the curriculum.
○ Mention high or rising standards and the school's determination to aim for the best.
○ Emphasize extra-curricular or enrichment opportunities.
○ Stress anything about the school which makes it distinctive (marketing experts call these unique selling points or USPs).
○ Keep the language crisp.
○ Consider offering the prospectus in other languages if that is likely to be useful in your area. Existing parents may be able to help with translations.
○ Think about the format – a booklet is one alternative or you might opt, as many schools now do, for a printed folder containing loose sheets. This is very easy and economical to update from year to year.

There are certain things your secondary school prospectus must by law also include.

○ School's name, address and phone number.
○ Type of school.
○ Headteacher's name.
○ Name of chair of governors.
○ Ethos statement.
○ Religious denomination or affiliation, if applicable.

- A note on the parents' right to withdraw their pupil from religious education and collective worship.
- Information on special educational needs (SEN) provision.
- The total number of pupils on roll.
- Last year's attendance and absence statistics.
- Last year's Key Stage SATs results.
- Last year's GCSE, AS-/A2-level, VCE and GNVQ results.
- Student destinations.

Materials for the school website

A school website should:

- include full contact details, including postal address and phone number, prominently and easily accessible. It is surprising how many school websites omit or obscure this essential detail
- state the full name of the headteacher: Mrs Irene Jacobson, Miss Mo Smith or Ian Grove
- publish a list of staff and their roles
- contain everything which is in the prospectus
- exploit the medium by including, say, a virtual tour or an example of the school band playing
- avoid dense blocks of text which very few people will read on screen
- use small chunks of text with plenty of pictures
- feature work by students, such as art or projects
- give school news, such as results of matches, awards won, funding achieved, new buildings underway or details of interesting visits and events
- be regularly updated
- be a creative and informative shop window for the school.

The school magazine

Editing or writing for the school magazine can be a good development task for any teacher interested in writing for publication. Although it's an in-house publication, it may also be sent to parents, given to visitors and circulated throughout the school's wider community. Typically an annual school magazine is published in the autumn term referring to the events of the previous school year. Use it to:

- say hello or goodbye to staff who have just started or just left
- report on the school's academic results and achievements
- publish accounts, preferably by students, of all the school's sport, drama and music activities
- celebrate school visits and trips with accounts by participants
- publish the best work of departments such as English and art
- put a really fine piece of student art on the cover each year
- list and celebrate the destinations on last year's leavers
- give news of former students
- publish as many photographs of school activities as possible
- develop student media skills by involving them in every possible way – from Year 7 upwards
- provide a 'real task' for GNVQ students who may be able to design and print it in school
- involve as many students and staff as possible in the planning, writing, design and production processes.

Writing for the school intranet

The intranet is a comprehensive, electronic noticeboard and virtual, communal filing cabinet for the school. Parts of it (e.g. pupil reports) are accessible only to staff, but much of it can usefully be available to pupils. Enlightened schools also make areas accessible – via a password – to pupils and parents at home and elsewhere. The intranet, which must be updated daily to work properly, could feature:

○ current notices such as 'Today's Year 11 after-school football practice is cancelled' or 'Today is the final day for entries in the English department's short story competition'
○ the school timetable
○ school policies
○ term dates
○ names and department of staff, with email addresses if you have the technology to make these available to pupils and parents
○ dates of events such as matches, concerts, parents' evenings, etc.
○ timetables for both public and internal examinations
○ invitations such as: 'Mrs Jones is prepared to start a French clinic in the lunch hour for anyone who would like extra help. Speak to Mrs Jones (Room 32, pkjones@anysecondary.dorset.school.uk or put a message in her pigeonhole) if you're interested'
○ art work by pupils – cartoons work well
○ anything you can think of to encourage pupils to refer to it regularly, such as a joke of the day.

Some secondary schools publish all their lesson-by-lesson programmes of study for all subjects on their intranet. It enables students and parents to see exactly what has been covered and where the course is going. It also helps pupils to catch up if they have missed lessons and presents parents with a very business-like and systematic image of curriculum planning.

L I S T 90 **Press releases**

All secondary schools need a good relationship with the press, especially locally. It's a key part of building a good reputation. Local papers and radio stations are usually prepared to publicize your achievements and activities in a much more positive way than national newspapers. Keep your local media informed by sending (preferably by email) press releases giving a brief account of what you want them to know about.

- ○ Be brief and incisive.
- ○ Restrict yourself to one side of A4 paper or the email equivalent.
- ○ Answer the traditional journalistic questions of who, what, why, where and when.
- ○ Include a contact name at the school and a phone number. If a journalist needs more information he or she will expect to ring and get through to someone who can help without delay or fuss.

Two general points about dealing with the media.

- ○ Don't try to tell a newspaper or radio station what to do. If they decide to feature your event, they are doing you a favour – not the other way round.
- ○ Remember that journalists are human beings with babies and bills to pay – like teachers but even less well paid. When you meet or speak to them treat them politely and don't assume that every hack is like the tiny minority which gets the profession a bad name.

Moving On, Out or Up 12

LIST 91 Reasons for leaving a school

- Retirement.
- Moving abroad (perhaps because of your partner's work).
- Relocating to another part of the UK.
- Downshifting.
- Sideways move to another school to widen experience (e.g. to teach post-16 or mixed sex).
- Promotion to another school.
- Teaching abroad for a year through organizations such as VSO.
- Time out to improve qualifications, e.g. study full time for a Master's degree.
- Career break, perhaps to raise a family.
- Moving to an education-related job, such as an LEA adviser or museum education officer.
- Ill health.
- Moving to a non-education job, such as starting your own business or becoming an HGV driver.
- Retraining for a different job, such as nursing or law.
- Feeling that the time is right. Secondary schools have a natural seven-year student cycle from Year 7 to Year 13. Staff sometimes feel it too.
- So fed up with teaching that even unemployment looks attractive!

Promotion routes

There are many secondary school opportunities above the level of basic classroom teaching.

- Headteacher/ headmistress/headmaster/principal/chief executive
- Deputy headteacher
- Assistant headteacher
- Head of specialism (e.g. sports, technology or music college) if the school has specialist status
- Head of department
- Deputy head of department
- Head of faculty
- Deputy head of faculty
- Head of year/year tutor
- Head of house
- Head of Key Stage 3/ Key Stage 4/post-16
- Deputy head of Key Stage 3/ Key Stage 4/ post-16
- Director of studies
- Examinations officer
- Special needs coordinator (SENCO)
- Gifted and talented (G&T) coordinator
- CPD coordinator
- Careers director
- Advanced skills teacher.

There is a new, but growing, trend for secondary schools to federate – that means two or more schools are formally linked – usually because one of the schools has weaknesses that will be rectified through working closely with a more successful school. Each school has its own headteacher whose line manager is the director or chief executive of the federation. It's another possible line of promotion for headteachers who might aim for a leadership role in a federation. The head of the federation is typically a former headteacher of one of the participating schools.

LIST 93 Promotion within the school

There are good reasons to seek promotion within your existing school.

○ You are already familiar with its culture.
○ As a 'home grown' product you are more likely to fit in.
○ You know the school's strengths and weaknesses and what needs to be done.
○ Your reputation goes before you.
○ Too much change is bad for the stability of the school and students' education.
○ You owe it loyalty.
○ You don't have to move house and/or uproot your family.
○ The first steps on the ladder are often more readily achieved after the NQT year if you remain in the same school where senior managers know what you can do.
○ It is less disruptive and stressful.

A generation ago it was almost unheard of for a secondary headteacher to be selected from the school's existing staff. Today the internal appointment of headteachers is surprisingly common.

LIST 94 Promotion elsewhere

Sometimes it can make sense to move to another school for promotion.

○ You can make a fresh start.
○ You bring ideas and contacts from your old school to your new one.
○ It is sometimes easier to exert authority and influence if you are a newcomer.
○ You avoid having to manage colleagues who have previously been peers – which is potentially tricky.
○ You leave your mistakes behind.
○ It is healthier for schools to have a regular influx of 'new blood' with experience of good practice.
○ No one should stay in the same workplace for too long.
○ It is challenging and enjoyable to 'learn the ropes' in a different school.

LIST 95 Education-related alternatives to teaching

You could consider using your teaching background and skills without actually having to prepare lessons and write student reports. There is a range of options.

- Becoming an Ofsted inspector (if you can live with the 'poacher turned gamekeeper' quips of your colleagues).
- Marking exams, e.g. SATs, GCSE, AS-/A2-level, VCE, etc.
- Consultancy.
- Administrative work for the LEA or another education provider.
- Advisory work.
- Student textbook writing.
- Writing online materials for students and/or teachers.
- Managing/editing an education website.
- Teacher training.
- Leading courses for teachers and schools.
- Working as an education officer for a charity, orchestra, heritage site, etc.
- Marketing or selling education materials.
- Becoming a classroom assistant (a surprising number are former teachers).

LIST 96 External applications for teaching posts

Job hunting beyond the available posts in your own school can be an exhilarating (even addictive!) experience from which you can learn a lot, even if you don't get the first position you apply for. Make your search systematic and regard it as a journey. You might find posts advertised in *The TES*, *SecEd*, the *Guardian*, an LEA circular or elsewhere, or you might hear about one informally, by word of mouth.

○ Send, phone or email for further details.
○ Find out what you can about the school. Websites are very useful, especially if the school is outside your area.
○ If you are offered the chance to have an informal telephone chat with someone at the school at this stage, take it.
○ Make sure your application or covering letter sets out simply, but pointedly, the ways in which you are fitted for the post.
○ Include anything else the school has asked for, such as names of referees, your 500-word solution to a given problem, a photograph.
○ Tell your present headteacher immediately and in confidence that you have applied – you have to give them as one of your referees and it will go against you if the first indication is a letter from the other school asking for a reference.
○ Remember, headteachers often phone each other for an off-the-record word about job applicants too.
○ Be prepared to hear nothing – many schools now acknowledge applications only if the applicant is selected for interview.
○ If the school invites you for a preliminary visit, take up the offer – the more information you have the better.
○ Arrive punctually and appropriately dressed for the interview and other selection procedures, such being asked to teach an observed lesson or chair a meeting.
○ Be positive about interviews even if you don't get the job. Regard them as a good opportunity to explore another school – a form of CPD.

LIST 97 Jobs to consider if you really have had enough

Teaching is an eclectic profession with highly transferable skills. If you can teach in a secondary school you probably also have what it takes to be a:

- ○ bookmaker
- ○ guest-house proprietor
- ○ publican
- ○ night-club manager
- ○ bouncer
- ○ negotiator
- ○ taxi driver
- ○ shop manager
- ○ police officer
- ○ social worker
- ○ bus driver
- ○ counsellor
- ○ tour guide
- ○ diplomat
- ○ bank clerk
- ○ paramedic
- ○ actor
- ○ after-dinner speaker.

L I S T **Serving notice**
98

So you're moving on and your notice is in.

○ Pupils should hear about your impending departure from you and no one else.

○ Make this clear to colleagues – pre-empt information leaks.

○ Don't get 'demob happy' and slacken your efforts during your last weeks – pupils and colleagues are still entitled to your best.

○ Try to avoid tactlessly asking for time off to visit your new school – fit it in after hours.

○ Don't walk about school beaming gleefully – it antagonizes envious colleagues!

○ Don't preface every remark with 'At (name of new school) they ...'

○ Be gracious about any parties and 'leaving dos' arranged for you.

○ Accept gifts from colleagues, governors, students and/or parents with grace.

○ Consider 'farewell' gestures of your own, such as a chocolate bar for every pupil you teach and/or a small personal wrapped gift for each member of the department or team you're leaving. This can work wonders in terms of spreading goodwill.

○ Send handwritten letters of thanks to all present-givers and party-arrangers.

LIST 99   What to take with you when you leave

Remember that once you have left a school you will never have access to its cupboards, intranet, shelves and filing cabinets again. If you go back you will be a visitor. So, gather up and take:

○ All lesson plans. Even if you're retiring you might decide to do a bit of private coaching or supply work in the future.
○ A copy of any document you've written.
○ Copies of any other work you have done for the school which you might ever wish to re-use, adapt or refer to.
○ Any books and other resources which belong to you personally – if you've been in post some time a surprising number will have found their way to your workplace.
○ Dog-eared copies of textbooks which you've been using for years, now so heavily annotated that they will never be any use to anyone else.
○ The contents of your locker.
○ Personal property in and on your desk.
○ Group photographs of colleagues, pupils and of your classroom and office – one can get quite sentimental about these in time. Take a camera to school in the last week – but be mindful of any rules your school has about photographing students.
○ Anything 'incriminating' which you don't want found after your departure, such as that hate letter you got from a Year 8 pupil in your first year at the school!

Maintaining links

Every school you teach in is one in which you have put down roots. Of course you are moving on and it isn't sensible to return too soon or too often, but there will be colleagues you want to keep in touch with and, particularly if you've retired, you might be invited to:

○ attend concerts and plays
○ support at sports events
○ help out on trips
○ give a talk
○ help with an after-school club
○ attend awards ceremonies
○ speak at an awards ceremony as a guest
○ give an assembly
○ share staff social occasions
○ judge competitions.

It would be a churlish person who didn't sometimes accept some of these invitations. And don't forget to send former schools a Christmas card when the time comes round.

If you're in a new school you might also invite some of your former colleagues to events there. Links work both ways.

L I S T 101   **Former pupils**

The TES runs a weekly slot, 'My best teacher' in which someone reasonably well known talks about a former teacher who has had an ongoing influence on his or her progress. Most of them have remained in touch with the teacher. That warmth and mutual respect is part of what keeps teachers going when battle fatigue threatens – especially at secondary level because the pupils are children when they arrive and young adults when they leave. I still get letters, Christmas cards, graduation, wedding and baby pictures – and more recently emails – from former pupils in three different schools.

When you and/or a pupil you've worked with closely leaves the school:

○ forget any sense of 'us and them'
○ give him or her your address, phone number and email address
○ trust that none of it will be abused – it rarely is
○ let the student make the choice. If you don't hear, then leave it at that
○ if a student contacts you, always respond
○ tell her or him what you're doing as well as commenting on what they've said
○ once a student has left school invite the use of your first name – it puts the relationship on a new footing
○ remember that learning of former pupils' successes is one of the great joys of teaching.

Printed in the USA
CPSIA information can be obtained
at www.ICGtesting.com
LVHW020846171024
794056LV00002B/427